Empowering Underrepresented Students in Science

STEM Students Speak

Empowering Underrepresented Students in Science

STEM Students Speak

Sonji Johnson-Anderson
Ranjana Lingutla
Margaret (Peg) Riley

ELSEVIER

AP

ACADEMIC PRESS
An imprint of Elsevier

Academic Press is an imprint of Elsevier
125 London Wall, London EC2Y 5AS, United Kingdom
525 B Street, Suite 1650, San Diego, CA 92101, United States
50 Hampshire Street, 5th Floor, Cambridge, MA 02139, United States
The Boulevard, Langford Lane, Kidlington, Oxford OX5 1GB, United Kingdom

Notices
Knowledge and best practice in this field are constantly changing. As new research and experience broaden our understanding, changes in research methods, professional practices, or medical treatment may become necessary.

Practitioners and researchers must always rely on their own experience and knowledge in evaluating and using any information, methods, compounds, or experiments described herein. In using such information or methods they should be mindful of their own safety and the safety of others, including parties for whom they have a professional responsibility.

To the fullest extent of the law, neither the Publisher nor the authors, contributors, or editors, assume any liability for any injury and/or damage to persons or property as a matter of products liability, negligence or otherwise, or from any use or operation of any methods, products, instructions, or ideas contained in the material herein.

British Library Cataloguing-in-Publication Data
A catalogue record for this book is available from the British Library.

Library of Congress Cataloging-in-Publication Data
A catalog record for this book is available from the Library of Congress.

ISBN: 978-0-323-90469-8

For Information on all Academic Press publications
visit our website at https://www.elsevier.com/books-and-journals

Publisher/Acquisitions Editor: Katey Birtcher
Editorial Project Manager: Alice Grant
Publishing Services Manager: Deepthi Unni
Project Manager: Radjan Lourde Selvanadin
Cover Designer: Ryan Cook

Typeset by MPS Limited, Chennai, India

Printed in the United States of America

Last digit is the print number: 9 8 7 6 5 4 3 2 1

Contents

Preface

It is vitally important to educate and prepare a highly qualified and diverse science, technology, engineering, and math (STEM) workforce. Our world depends on it. The overall economy, to say nothing of the health system, agriculture, and technology sectors, all rely upon STEM innovation. Diversity drives innovation and a lack of it results in our inability to harness the full potential of our STEM workforce. In an increasingly complex world, it is critical that all of our nation's youth have the opportunity to acquire the skills and knowledge to solve problems and learn how to work in teams, as they gather and make sense of evidence. Given its obvious critical value to our nation's health and prosperity, one might suppose that in the US, we would have already developed the most effective, engaging, and inclusive approaches to STEM education. While we may not lead the world in math performance, we do invest tens of millions of dollars each year in STEM educational innovation. Clearly, there should be no need to address this issue: If we just educate our students, innovation will follow.

If only it were that simple. More than three million STEM jobs will go unfilled in 2021 alone. Couple that with a severe underrepresentation of women and people of color in STEM industries, and the problem comes into full view. Only half of college students majoring in STEM fields will graduate and pursue a career in STEM, and even fewer will be underrepresented minorities (URMs). We have, indeed, invested tens of millions in STEM education, innovation, and retention efforts, and yet, we have not significantly moved the needle; half of our STEM students simply give up in their STEM educational pursuits. For some, it is the cold, sterile environment of many STEM classrooms that turns them away; others don't see themselves represented in most STEM professions and their instructors, often white males, reinforce this observed lack of diversity; and yet more are told early on that they don't have "what it takes" to make it in STEM fields.

This book attempts to answer the question of why we have had such a lack of success in engaging and retaining a diverse body of STEM students. Here, we chronicle our journey creating the STEM Ambassadors Program, a retention program designed to provide a supportive, inclusive community that welcomes and embraces the diversity of our STEM college students. STEM Ambassadors provides key educational support, professional skills development, and culturally aware activities. It is a community our students have embraced and over which they have taken ownership. The program provides robust and multifaceted support with mentoring and community building woven throughout. The STEM Ambassadors Program, or simply "STEM AP," as our students have named it, focuses on building students' science identity, strengthening their leadership skills, providing rich research experiences, and nurturing their overall sense of self-efficacy.

Here, we relate how we created this community and describe the tools, resources, and activities we employ to ensure our students thrive. As we chronicle the development of STEM AP, we also amplify the voices of our students as they recount their experiences in the program. Together, we have created a diverse, rich, and thriving community, undergirded by our belief in the value of students' identities and experiences. We also assert that the methods we have employed are absolutely reproducible and could prove useful to those seeking to provide support for, or to diversify, other STEM professional and learning spaces.

We believe what we have created a viable pathway to retaining underrepresented students in STEM. We also believe that the answer to the question posed above—why we have had such poor success in engaging and retaining a diverse body of STEM students in the US—is that, until now, many of us have focused our efforts single-mindedly on defining, developing, and refining specific retention practices, ensuring students have access to them, and, hopefully, tracking the student outcomes. These are certainly all essential activities. However, with this intense focus on the mechanics of our approaches, many of us have forgotten something even more basic that our students want—in fact, crave—from us as educators. They need us to listen, to take the time to hear what they have to say, and to respond directly to those concerns and desires. Yes, our students want research experiences and benefit immensely from mentoring. However, what has become lost in this race to retain is the simple fact that our students, first and foremost, need to be heard.

There came a moment in our efforts to create STEM Ambassadors, particularly as we took the time to read our students' reflections, when we realized we had lost our way. We had become so focused on providing every possible resource for our students and creating complicated spreadsheets to track their progress that we forgot this most basic element: we forgot to ask the students what they wanted from us. It was at that moment that we made a conscious decision to stop what we were doing and start listening. The impact on ourselves, our students, and our program was astounding.

With this in mind, we invite you to listen to our students as they describe the challenges they face in their STEM educational journeys and how our program has helped them hone their inner fortitude to overcome the hurdles, maneuver past the roadblocks, and develop confidence in their own abilities to succeed. In the end, listening to our students was the key to building a successful STEM retention program. Further, we believe that this may be the single most important thing one can do to ensure that the greatest diversity of students succeed in their STEM studies. We encourage everyone to make a conscious effort to listen more closely to their students (or employees), and invite them to share what they need to feel part of the diverse, productive, and engaging classroom, community of scholars, or workforce that you hope to achieve. You may be surprised by what you hear. We certainly were.

Acknowledgments

It has been exciting to witness the metamorphosis of the STEM Ambassadors Program. Many scholars, students, and staff have contributed to this project, providing brainpower, time, and talent to create a highly successful program that effectively serves its students. As part of our community, we thank those who have gone above and beyond for the success of our students.

STEM AP was first envisioned by Prof. Riley nearly ten years ago. After several attempts to translate that vision into reality, STEM AP was the recipient of a prestigious and very generous award from the UMass President's Office. Provost John McCarthy (then Dean of the Graduate School) took a chance on our unproven ideas and provided the administrative support required to garner the program's initial funds. The next 3 years saw a flurry of activity, as we engaged STEM education experts, STEM faculty, and several hundred students. With each passing month, we learned more about what our students needed to succeed in their STEM studies. Once we felt we were truly on the right path, we developed a proposal for the National Science Foundation. For this, we thank our team of scholars, in particular Dr. Ally Hunter, who worked tirelessly for the grant proposal process that successfully won a million-dollar award from the NSF, which provided program funding up to our final session on 15 March 2021. We gratefully acknowledge the support of NSF's Division of Undergraduate Education (NSF DUE-1726808).

We thank Dr. Carolyn Gardner-Thomas for her vision and direction, which enabled STEM AP to rebrand itself as a supportive, purposeful, and focused counterspace/community of scientists. We are also grateful to the many lab PI's who provided internship and mentorship opportunities for our student participants throughout the years. We are indebted to the university and community of scholars who committed time and resources to present at our Monday night seminars, as well as our amazing group of graduate mentors who continue to serve with commitment and dedication.

STEM AP was housed in the Department of Biology in the College of Natural Sciences at UMass Amherst, and we thank the faculty and staff for all the help and resources they made available to our program over the years. Our most precious resource, by far, has been our extraordinary students who served as both community participants and program staff. Their creativity, consistency, and collective genius in shaping and helping the program grow, and in aiding their own social and scholastic achievements cannot be overstated.

Our students, past and present, have been the lifeblood of this work. Some of them have shared their personal experiences in this book. We thank all those who have, in any way, contributed to the creation and sustenance of the STEM Ambassadors Program. Lastly, we thank our readers for taking the time to experience our journey and learn from the invaluable wisdom, challenges, and lessons we've garnered along the way.

About the Authors

Sonji Johnson-Anderson is the director of the UMass Amherst STEM Ambassadors Program. Sonji's research interests sit at the intersection of Black Feminist Epistemology, Critical Race Theory, and Performance Ethnography. Her work focuses on the experiences of students and families who are marginalized in public domains, primarily educational institutions. A gifted educator and public speaker, Sonji brings decades of teaching experience and a deep commitment to critical and culturally relevant pedagogy. She also serves as a researcher with the 7 Generation Movement Collective LLC, an Amherst-based community engagement consultancy that works in tandem with community groups and large and small organizations to investigate issues of diversity and inclusion to enact change that is socially just and equitable.

Ranjana Lingutla is a medical student at the Tufts University School of Medicine. She earned her bachelor's in Biochemistry and Molecular Biology from the University of Massachusetts Amherst in 2020. A native of Western Massachusetts, she has devoted her time to mentoring students from traditionally marginalized backgrounds through various public-school systems and community organizations. In 2016, she was recruited to the STEM Ambassadors Program to serve as a mentoring instructor, after which she was selected to be the undergraduate program manager and assistant director. With a passion for furthering education and providing equal opportunity, she continues to support underrepresented students in STEM communities through mentorship and sharing their stories.

Margaret (Peg) Riley is a professor in the Department of Biology at the University of Massachusetts Amherst. She received her PhD from Harvard and served 15 years on the Yale faculty before moving to UMass in 2012. Peg's research focuses on the evolution of antibiotic resistance and the use of ecologically sound approaches to drug discovery. She is one of the pioneers of narrow-spectrum antimicrobials, which provide novel solutions to the global challenge of antibiotic resistance. She is passionate about engaging the public in science, having created the Massachusetts Academy of Sciences and serving as its founding president for five years, and devotes considerable energy to ensuring her students can relate their scientific discoveries to their own lives and challenges.

Chapter 1

Who Needs STEM Support?

Introduction

"Maybe it's not for you!" These were the words one of the university's distinguished STEM professors said to an overwhelmed, doubt-ridden freshman. Words that moved her to quit STEM... only, she didn't! Thankfully, fate (or serendipity) stepped in when she met the director of the STEM Ambassadors Program (STEM AP), who gave her an entirely different perspective, and she persevered.

"If it wasn't for this program, I would have changed my major," Carmen, one of our STEM Ambassadors, remarked pointedly. With eyes shining and a smile that brightened the room, Carmen continued to speak of the isolation and the uncertainty; the overwhelming, crushing doubt she experienced as a freshman STEM major. She then described meeting our program's director and how this brief encounter changed her world! The director quickly disabused Carmen of the notion that she couldn't "make it" in STEM and encouraged her to join STEM AP. With the support and encouragement of our community, Carmen persisted in her STEM studies and became an outstanding student leader in our program. Her goal was to go on to medical school, an ambition she pursued with passion and resolve. Gone were the feelings of doubt, replaced with a strong sense of her own STEM identity, and the certainty that she had much to offer the world!

Carmen's story—or at least the start of it—is sadly a common one. Students arrive at college passionate about being a doctor, a research scientist, a veterinarian—or one of many other STEM professionals—and then quickly become overwhelmed. Their classes are large and unwelcoming, they feel that they have to rely on their own resources to succeed, and they often have a hard time making new friends. Doubts emerge, fester, and grow until half of our most talented students simply give up—or, worse yet, are *encouraged* to give up by an unthinking faculty advisor—before they have even been truly able to give STEM studies a chance.

We will return to Carmen's journey and introduce you to the stories of many more STEM Ambassadors as we chronicle how our program was created and then transformed by the very students we had sought to help. These students took ownership of STEM AP and showed us, the presumed leaders, what they

Empowering Underrepresented Students in Science. DOI: http://dx.doi.org/10.1016/B978-0-323-90469-8.00001-9

really needed. And what they needed looked very different from what we had initially incorporated into our program. The quick take-home message of this story is that students spoke, we listened, and magic happened!

The Value of the STEM Community

Scholars have long waxed eloquent about the value of diverse understandings and perspectives in STEM.[1] But what really is this diversity in STEM about which we speak so glibly? For instance, what should be done to ensure there is an increased presence of Black and Brown faces in a science classroom? How do we get more students from homes of lower socioeconomic status to learn alongside their more moneyed peers? What should we do to ensure more students who learn differently achieve excellence in their scholarship? How may we engage students who identify as LGBTQIA+ to feel as much a part of the STEM educational space as anyone else? What can we do to provide students whose parents or relatives have never been to college with the opportunity to do so? What should college and university programs do to help such students acquire the learning and career opportunities they need to excel? Again, smooth answers abound: advise them; give them research opportunities; assign them a mentor; or provide tutors. We have invested hundreds of millions of dollars in the design and operation of such well-intentioned, supportive programs.

But if this is essentially all supporting diversity in STEM means, then what do we do with these diverse students once we get them seated beside each other in classrooms? So much of what is done in diversity-enhancing programs has been reified and commoditized; too frequently, it only serves the purpose of checking off boxes and doing for the sake of doing, simply to keep pace with the trends. We agree that to diversify any college classroom, if only for its own sake, is to add richness and texture to the learning experience of every student seated in that class. But how do we move from merely having students from differing backgrounds who happened to register for the same course to nurturing a community of learners who are open, respectful, and valuing of each other's perspectives? How do we get these students and their professors to embrace, even desire, to locate themselves in diverse learning communities, not just because these communities are aesthetically pleasing, or trendy, but because scholars understand such learning spaces hold the key to real discovery of solutions to real-world problems? How do we move beyond the symbolic act of inclusion and diversification to a clear and deep understanding and a focused and sustained advocacy for its ubiquity? Of what value is a reflexive, robust apprehension of the benefits of STEM diversity?

The STEM Ambassadors Community

There is energy and electricity in the room. *"Wonder what they are going to do with us this week!"* is the question on these young people's minds as they gather with anticipation inside our new location, freshly expanded because of the growing number of students in our program. In response to this demand, we created an "open to all" marketplace of sorts for the production and bartering of ideas, a place where we can address the myriad issues students face each week as STEM scholars. And, as important as those issues are to deal with per and among students, it is the resulting cohesive community that is the crowning achievement of this weekly gathering.

One of the foci of our program is a weekly STEM seminar, which is inspired by the knowledge that nothing validates or humanizes a person more than the opportunity to meet others as members of the same community whose stories, experiences, and identities matter. And it's not just that these things matter; it's that they are central to our students' understanding of themselves and each other, and to their success in their respective programs.

To flourish in STEM, scholars need more than simply STEM training, STEM knowledge, STEM experience, and STEM role models; they need *all* the training, knowledge, experience, and role models possible, and the expertise of everyone and everything they have ever done: STEM and non-STEM! It is, therefore, important to encourage students to embrace their unique identities and claim those crucial, treasured, and inseparable components of themselves as fundamental to the formation of their professional, intellectual, and personal selves. Scientists with a holistic view of the world; scientists with an inclusive understanding of humanity; scientists who value the totality of their life experiences, having learned from them all—the mundane as well as the spectacular—are scientists to whom we may entrust our future, whose inquiry and curiosity about our world could lead us to deeper discoveries and understanding of ourselves as a species.

This is what a STEM support program ought to do for the students it serves. Ultimately, all of our endeavors, decisions, actions, or inactions are connected. Scientists and artists alike save lives. Their discoveries and creations save us from ourselves, and often, if not always, from giving in to our worst, most hateful or destructive impulses. STEM support, therefore, should not be construed as a "training wheels" program for those in science who are most at risk for failure, but as a kind of deprogramming for STEM students, a way of redirecting them to themselves, so they get to see how crucial their embrace and understanding of their whole being is to their own success in the field.

Thus, to be a good scientist, one's science must be infused with all of one's self. To fully understand and be able to firmly stand in the self as a scientist, one must use the resources of *all* of one's experiences, but one must be taught how to do this; one must be taught how to make meaning of one's own experiences and, in that process, develop a science identity!

Despite the inherent diversity of the students we support, there are inherent similarities, too. One of the most powerful is also one of the most prevalent: Once they get a taste of what it is like to embrace themselves, wholly and fully, there seems to be no stopping them. This enthusiasm, this clarity of self and purpose, is the essence of what a STEM support program ought to yield in the students it serves. Students learn to see themselves as scientists, capable of creating change in their world; they learn how to communicate their science and connect with the people they serve and serve with; they embrace and value themselves, mistakes, missteps, and all. They recognize the struggle others endure and they see themselves in the struggles and stories of others. All in all, they learn to be human while doing science!

The Power of Mentoring

Ciara is an African-American female student in our program. She had endured some significant health challenges during the prior school year and returned to classes with physical evidence of her trauma in tow. We worried that she would not return to us at all, given that she was now physically hampered. But no sooner than Ciara set foot on campus, she reported to our office, ready to engage in another semester of community building and learning. She even opted to get more involved by becoming a middle school mentor.

"Middle school mentoring was one of my favorite experiences [this past] semester. I really enjoyed the interactions with the students in my group and realized that I could learn a lot from them," she reflected. Ciara was taken aback by the discovery of how "stuck" and "boxed in" her own thought processes were when she had to find ways to get through to her middle school mentees about science. This experience opened her eyes to the limits she had placed around her own actual "doing" of science. Beyond learning how to keep a group of energetic youngsters interested in the activity at hand, she also uncovered how to approach science itself in different ways. This was a defining experience for Ciara, one that made her step back from herself, seeing herself and how she had defined herself as a scientist with new eyes. The reflexive process was awakened in her, boosting her to a new level of awareness as a scholar.

Mentoring relationships, like the one Ciara formed with local middle schoolers, form the fabric of our community. For example, small groups of first-year students meet weekly with peer mentors to build friendships and explore college life. As another student, Janet, noted, "It was nice to be surrounded by fellow STEM majors who understand the difficulty of the courses you are taking. I have a good feeling about my group and know that it will be very beneficial to me throughout the year." Edward was even more effusive: "[I]t is easy to say that my near-peer mentor was for sure the main reason I had such an awesome academic week."

These same students are also introduced to graduate student mentors who help them learn about the process of engaging in research. The graduate mentors work with their younger mentees to develop essential research skills. They read scientific articles together; learn how to design well-controlled experiments; and visit research labs, all while cultivating and nourishing these critical relationships. Spring, a first-year student, noted, "This week I was also introduced to my graduate mentor, who was super nice! He spoke about his research and gave us pointers and advice, which are super helpful! Through these activities, I am more confident in my future and know how to approach professors and what I need to accomplish before the end of this year."

Laura was a sunny but shy presence when she first enrolled in our program as a freshman. She didn't participate much at the beginning, but it was clear she was interested in the activities we offered. Laura won one of the coveted STEM AP Summer Research Experiences for Undergraduates (REU), which introduced her to working in a lab. The experience of being on campus during the summer with a small, intimate group of students from her program drew her out of herself. By the end of the summer, Laura had developed spunk to pair with her smiles! This experience pushed her to try middle school mentoring during the following semester.

Laura learned the importance of communicating one's science clearly through her experience as a middle school mentor. "If you cannot communicate your research to people who are perhaps not experts or who know very little on the topic, you will not get your point across," she asserted, "nor will you inspire someone to care about your research." The experience made her grow as a communicator of science. "I think middle school mentoring has helped me become a better communicator and has made me feel more confident in my abilities and [science] knowledge." And although she experienced some initial self-doubt—remarking that "… I was so anxious they would ask me questions I did not know the answers to… or be uninterested in the projects we were doing, just general fears that I would be awkward… I wanted to do well!"—she gained a strong sense of confidence from her mentoring experience. She also learned something important about engaging the whole of the students under her charge: "It was so nice to get to know them all, to see their talents outside of the projects we were doing for [that] day, and to see them get more comfortable with me as the sessions went on."

Building a STEM Identity Through Reflection

If asked why they chose to study science, we would bet that most STEM students would say they hope to find solutions to the world's many challenges; curing disease, fighting climate change, building safer buildings, or simply gaining knowledge about ourselves and our planet. Every student who has had this desire, or who has harbored a curiosity or a dream about providing solutions that seek to advance our species, is a student worthy of respect. And every student with this noble desire deserves to comprehensively understand the value of his or her scholarship to the overall betterment of human existence. Such a world view, such an ontological perspective, must, therefore, come from those positioned to most consequentially influence students' understanding of their work and its value to society, as well as to themselves as members of the human family.

This is where we begin in our STEM AP to deviate from the beaten track of popular rhetoric about STEM diversity. We *reflect* with our students not just about their ambitions and career goals (important as those are). We *reflect* with them about their connections to other human beings. We *reflect* with them about the value of their experiences—challenges, setbacks, comebacks, all of it—and help them link the value of their journey to the understanding of themselves as they currently are, where they stand *today* in light of how far they have traveled. Of what value are these reflections other than to awaken past pains or relive old victories? Reflection leads students into a place of self-reflexivity, self-understanding, and self-affirmation. It promotes in them a doing of science from a place of clarity. When they can share the stories and the experiences of their varied peers and come to expect and desire variety, they arrive at a connection to their own and others' conjoined humanity in a way they may not have grasped before.

It is only at this juncture of their multilayered awareness of purpose that students come to a readiness, a preparedness to *do* STEM! Our students begin to perceive and apply the practice of including as many voices, perspectives, backgrounds, and approaches as possible. They comprehend that only through this robust diversity can humanity truly benefit in a way that advances all our lives.

We have stated it repeatedly already, and we do so again: there is a woeful lack of diversity in STEM classrooms. And a lack of diversity in any classroom, in any space, especially in a multicultural society such as this one, is a loss to all in it. When students come to a learning space, they should arrive and engage with the knowledge that their presence and contribution are important. They should know that without their presence, the space and how those present experience it would be entirely different. We stress the importance of self-awareness in our program so that students will know who they are and that what they contribute to their learning community is of vital importance to its growth and advancement.

People generally assess their self-worth by the cues they get from members of their social group. Think about young people falling over themselves to be friends with their popular peers. In such environments, the popular youngsters are affirmed; they know they matter. These individuals know they are important because they are wholly affirmed by a society that endorses their particular looks or ways of being. Young people so approved move with a little more certainty and confidence in the world than do their less sanctioned counterparts. For them, the world is just a little safer, more reliable, and more accepting than it is for their peers. In such cases, they are not as challenged to make friends or command positive attention. This applies, too, where the development of a STEM identity is concerned. When students must fit themselves into an environment into which they are not readily perceived as belonging, the struggle to excel becomes even more difficult.

Unfortunately, for many students in STEM, this affirmation simply doesn't happen. Instead, for many diverse students, the norm is a negative assumption about who they are. It is an uphill climb just to be included. Sanchez Gibau[2] speaks of the "disruption" to the development of a student's science identity when a student believes their ability as a scientist is doubted by the institution or by "meaningful others" within it, such as professors. At its core, a STEM support program does what it says if it helps students navigate their way by advocating for them when they encounter specific challenges: connecting them with tutoring help, reaching out to professors if personal crises hit, providing them with mentorship, and so on. But a STEM support program does not fulfill its mandate if that is *all* it does. Students need to be empowered in the process to become their own most assertive and vociferous advocates. They must learn to see value in themselves and the unique worth they provide to their communities. They must be equipped with information about the demands of the world of research and industry and become appropriately prepared to take them on. Students should walk away from a support program strong, aware, confident, and informed enough to create their own circle of support for themselves and others. And while this may not necessarily be the stated aim of our particular program, it should definitely be one of the proofs of it.

Our program advocates what we call a "Reflexive Research Response," which is steeped in relationship- and community-building, reflection on self and others' experiences, and the linking of self and others to one's own particular practice of science. In other words, STEM AP advocates for deep understanding, and for deep and self-conscious awareness of one's own purpose and direction. It hinges on the idea that the best scientists are the most self-aware and critically conscious ones. Self-reflection is a habit we work at building in our students, so that as they undergo the process of learning, they see why they are made to do what they do and how this contributes to their understanding of the purpose of our program; and ultimately, the purpose of their own lives. They do not always grasp this during their first weeks of participation. But over time, as they are made to both reflect out loud upon their weekly activities and to write about them, the value of their self-reflection becomes clearer.

"As a man thinketh, so is he" is a Biblical reference that speaks to the link between one's perception of self and *being* that which one perceives. In other words, a person cannot become more than what they perceive of themselves. In this context, if underrepresented STEM students do not think of themselves as scientists, there is no way they will become scientists! And they will not think of themselves as scientists as long as the science spaces they enter are not open and welcoming to their presence. This is why an investment in community building is so crucial to the process of STEM retention. By understanding who they are in the science space, the importance of their being there, and how to make meaning of the experiences they have there, students equip themselves to do more than just survive in this space; they thrive in it. They cannot accomplish this without self-reflection that leads to both general self-understanding and self-understanding as a scientist.

Becoming a Scientist by Doing Science

Let us state the obvious: one very significant way that students develop a science identity is by *doing science*. The more opportunities students get to experience themselves as scientists, the more they come to own who they are as scientists. Studies show that research experiences help students develop a sense of identity as STEM professionals by engaging in activities, such as designing their own studies, choosing experimental methods, and collecting data that are of intrinsic interest; all these activities encourage autonomy and allow for a greater sense of project ownership and contribute in no small part to a student's growing science identity.[3]

Unfortunately, most students—especially those of the demographic our program serves—generally do not get the chance to *do* authentic science to the extent they need, especially as undergraduates newly immersed in STEM learning. At the heart of this challenge is the simple fact that there are far more STEM students than there are research opportunities. For example, in the Biology Department at University of Massachusetts Amherst, there are 30 research active faculty and a student body of 1500. Unless every faculty member were to devote their entire lab effort to training undergraduates, only a mere 20% to 30% of our students would ever gain access to a research laboratory.

However, the challenge is even greater, and more insidious, than a simple lack of research opportunities. For the student demographic our program serves, the few available research opportunities too often pass by because students are simply unaware of the great importance of acquiring research experience or they don't know how to gain such experiences. In many instances, by the time students come to this awareness, they are nearing the end of their college tenure! Moreover, this shortfall compounds: for instance, a lack of research experience generally renders students less competitive than their more informed and prepared peers. Thus, the cycle perpetuates itself: the more resourced students get the more "plum" internships, setting them on the trajectory for admission into graduate school, medical school, or employment in competitive positions in industry. Such students (deemed successful) are generally also the least experienced in working in diverse communities. This could present a seemingly insurmountable challenge.

So where might we find a solution to this very real problem?

We found one in CUREs (Course-Based Undergraduate Research Experiences), which are class-based research immersions that provide students with authentic research experiences they would be otherwise hard-pressed to find. CUREs are designed to make STEM research meaningful, while also accommodating far more students than is possible in a standard research laboratory. Students often feel that the STEM topics they encounter in classes are inaccessible and irrelevant to their lives,[4] and the cookbook-like "lab classes" they attend only reinforce this sense of irrelevance. In contrast, in many CURES, students tackle personally selected problems with uncertain outcomes and feel that their work is respected precisely because they have generated new data. In this learning environment, students have the potential to learn a great deal more about the nature of research and about their own identities as investigators, which adds to their sense of belonging to the STEM community of researchers[5,6] and leads to persistence.[7]

A CURE stands in the gap and acts as a proxy for laboratory-based research experiences. A well-configured CURE, such as those our program offers, provides opportunities for students to collaborate with each other, ask questions and challenge each other and their instructor, and to make discoveries on their own while learning the hands-on practicality and applicability of the science being done. Students report that they love the team atmosphere and the work they get to do with their peers. They note that working together helps them rely on each other and trust what the other is doing, despite the urge of wanting to do things their own way.

For Jessie, a spunky first-year student, the CURE experience was truly engaging: "These activities are sparking my interest in the STEM field even more than before. The more involved I am becoming, the more I am fascinated and engaged, which is causing my desire to have a career in the STEM field to grow even more." For Santiago, it went even further: "Because I can say with complete confidence that this lab experience is one of the most fulfilling parts of my college life, it's a challenge I'm willing to unwaveringly embrace all day and night."

In the real world, be it academia or industry, STEM scholars must learn to collaborate, to work as part of a team, as much as they need to be self-directed and self-motivated to see tasks to their completion. A CURE doesn't just offer opportunities to investigate phenomena that are of interest; it also, as part of its process, builds upon a student's practical exposure to scientific inquiry; teaches research protocols; provides opportunities for collaboration and problem-solving; and develops students' leadership and communication skills, among several other pertinent skill sets. After participating in our CUREs, students often have the chance to present their research at local conferences, and through these opportunities, have received meaningful feedback from scholars who are experts in their field; some have also secured mentorships and internships and formed connections with other scholars in their field.

Bringing It All Together

Each of the topics we have addressed thus far—building a STEM identity, being engaged with a welcoming and supportive community, reflecting on one's self, having the opportunity to mentor and be mentored, and engaging in research experiences—is a key part of what has made STEM AP successful. However, STEM AP is far more than its constituent parts, and *that* is where the magic comes from. In subsequent chapters, you will learn about each of the component parts of STEM AP and, more importantly, you will hear from our students themselves about why these components matter. You will gain an understanding of how our students have transformed STEM AP from a fairly conventional STEM retention program into one from which emergent properties have appeared. What started out as a series of well-intentioned, carefully designed group activities has evolved into a complex and dynamic ecology of relationships, community building, skills development, research experiences, and more. We have had the pleasure of witnessing the transformation of an idea into a movement, one that is led by the students and for the students.

Our program thrives because our students want it to, and they are willing to put in their effort into ensuring that it flourishes. When we declare that this program has become a movement at our university, we are simply echoing what the students themselves say and write. Jose, one of our upper-class members, asserted, “STEM AP has been the highlight of this week for me. I believe God sent this program to help me maintain focus and I count this as the highlight of my semester. Everything I learn, I can incorporate into my life, so STEM AP is my life lesson class. It helps me remain focused on my goals and look forward to the places that I want to go to and the people that I want to meet and the person that I want to be in the future.”

Julia, a fairly shy senior, noted, “Leaving STEM AP feels like I have to leave my friends behind or as if I am moving away. The people have provided me with so many good memories that I can take with me forever. I not only laughed at the happy moments, but I also cried at all the sad ones. I have really connected with my roots over the year in this program. It has provided me with a lot of insight into what’s out there, and even my own capabilities. I am sad that I will not be able to continue this experience in my last semester, but I know that the journey does not stop here. STEM AP will always be a part of me, and thus it will always be a part of this world. Everything we have learned will be taken with us toward our future as we continue to succeed and make a difference in the world. I cannot wait to see how our hands mold the world of science in the future.”

And finally, Samantha, a relative newcomer to the program, described her gratitude for STEM AP. “One thing that I am really grateful for as a member of STEM AP is the countless number of students who serve as positive role models even without intending to. It’s really motivational being surrounded by students who are passionate about their studies and future careers. It motivates me to keep working hard and to not give up after encountering any obstacles.”

One might ask whether the program we are describing can be replicated in other contexts; our answer is a resounding yes! Certainly, as contexts vary, so would the needs and demands of those whom such a program serves. But what is of paramount importance is the fact that it is entirely possible to create and sustain programs like ours that do for their students immeasurably more than is thought to be possible. And programs that are absolutely affordable and sustainable if undergirded by the principles of equity, inclusivity, community, and reflection, and which use resources that target these outcomes, are the most effective, we believe, for underrepresented STEM scholars.

Scientists and science educators should seek to develop STEM retention programs for the purpose of diversifying science and rendering it more accessible and equitable, just as much as they attend to the advance of science and technology themselves. If science and scientists come only from small, homogenous swaths of society, then our science is immediately limited in its scope. These are all common-sense assertions, but unfortunately not ideas that permeate the heart of STEM spaces. As important as it is to present methods and means of access to encourage the marginalized in science, it is equally crucial to change the thinking and the perception of the gatekeepers of science so they critically apprehend the need for diversity in every area and aspect of science. We contend this diversification *must* happen if science is to flourish and provide the much-needed and sought-after answers and solutions to human suffering.

In the ensuing chapters, we attempt to show how our program has been able to accomplish the all-important task of creating a community of scientists that is warm, supportive, and engaging and which often sees students excelling well beyond their own expectations. Our secret is an open one, which we gladly share with you. Through our words and our students' voices, we invite you to experience the STEM AP!

References

1. Killpack, T. L.; Melón, L. C. Toward Inclusive STEM Classrooms: What Personal Role Do Faculty Play? *CBE Life Sci. Educ.* **2016**, *15* (3). DOI:10.1187/cbe.16-01-0020.
2. Gibau, G. S. Considering Student Voices: Examining the Experiences of Underrepresented Students in Intervention Programs. *CBE Life Sci. Educ.* **2015**, *14* (3), ar28. DOI:10.1187/cbe.14-06-0103.
3. Corwin, L. A.; Graham, M. J.; Dolan, E. L. Modeling Course-Based Undergraduate Research Experiences: An Agenda for Future Research and Evaluation. *CBE Life Sci. Educ.* **2015**, *14* (1), es1. DOI:10.1187/cbe.14-10-0167.
4. Barr, D. A.; Matsui, J.; Wanat, S. F.; Gonzalez, M. E. Chemistry Courses as the Turning Point for Premedical Students. *Adv. Health Sci. Educ.* **2010**, *15* (1), 45–54. DOI:10.1007/s10459-009-9165-3.
5. Johri, A.; Olds, B. M. Situated Engineering Learning: Bridging Engineering Education Research and the Learning Sciences. *J. Eng. Educ.* **2011**, *100* (1), 151–185. DOI:10.1002/j.2168-9830.2011.tb00007.x.
6. Pryor, J. H. *The American Freshman: National Norms, Fall 2009*; Higher Education Research Institute, University of California, 2009.
7. Estrada, M.; Woodcock, A.; Hernandez, P. R.; Schultz, P. W. Toward a Model of Social Influence That Explains Minority Student Integration Into the Scientific Community. *J. Educ. Psychol.* **2011**, *103* (1), 206–222. DOI:10.1037/a0020743.

Chapter 2

Building a STEM Identity

Why a STEM Identity Matters

To offer the best value within our increasingly diverse society, it is essential that our scientists, engineers, and mathematicians—indeed, all of the myriad STEM professionals—represent the full diversity of our community and world. Appropriately addressing problems, such as healing diseases, advancing technology, or solving engineering challenges, requires the skills and approaches of scientists from all backgrounds. It is, therefore, essential that STEM fields be diversified, regardless of how challenging this goal may be. It is for all our sakes that this is done.

However, the even trickier challenge lies in ensuring that when these diverse STEM professionals join forces, perhaps to create new vaccines, build a more efficient wind turbine, or develop more powerful machine learning algorithms, they are empowered and encouraged to bring all of themselves to the table. For only when we have a clear understanding and appreciation of our own unique talents, experiences, and knowledge will we fully harness the extraordinary power that diversity brings.

An identity is a "general sense of self with reference to groups or particular content,"[1] which means that it develops in relation to others. Thus, experiences in STEM educational settings, such as with instructors, research scientists, mentors, peers, and the materials employed in those settings, inform an individual's understanding of self.[2] Considerable research has emphasized that not all students feel welcome in STEM disciplines[3,4]—hence, the feeling of "otherness" our students experience as they enter their STEM majors.[5] Moreover, different students respond differently to our efforts to engage them; the process of triggering interest is nuanced by the particular activity and whether the learner is ready to respond.[1]

Developing students' STEM identity is critical because doing so creates a set of positive expectations that leads to more engaged learning.[2] When students have examples in their mind of individuals who have achieved professional success in their intended field, their excitement naturally propels them to take responsibility for what they're learning. Students take control of their learning because they are motivated by genuine interest. However, finding appropriate role models for women and minority students in STEM fields can

Empowering Underrepresented Students in Science. DOI: http://dx.doi.org/10.1016/B978-0-323-90469-8.00002-0

prove challenging.[6] Some of those we might imagine to be the most influential role models are, in fact, not Nobel Laureates, Silicon Valley entrepreneurs, neurosurgeons, or astronauts—in part because there are so few that look like our students. Rather, they are the fellow students, mentors, scientists, and teachers our students interact with daily. Unfortunately, these potential role models also only rarely look like our students—unless particular attention is paid to ensuring there is diversity in our classrooms.

The STEM Ambassadors Program (STEM AP) purposely addresses this need for students to develop their own STEM identities. To begin with, we engage students in exercises that encourage them to identify what makes them unique. We create opportunities for them to exchange stories that chronicle their struggles, their victories, and all they do to cope with the issues that challenge them. In giving voice to these stories, our students quickly learn that they are not alone in their feelings of "otherness," which contributes to the sense of connection they experience with each other. Students who connect in this way form friendships and create a robust, meaningful community. This community is the heart and soul of the STEM AP—and the reason it is so successful is because it is created *by* the students, not *for* them.

The students who participate in our program find community because they can relate to each other; they find friendships and share the pride of accomplishment. They feed off each other's successes, for they know when they see their peers succeed that they can, too. This is why building community is so essential to students' construction of a STEM identity. Having a community reinforces resilience, it encourages them to try and try again; it pulls them out of the doldrums of setbacks and difficulties and inspires them to use their trials and failures as learning experiences that catapult them to success.

The literature on science identity speaks to the need of STEM students to be recognized as scientists, in that they are able to show that they understand science content and possess the necessary skills marking them as competent, and able to demonstrate a fluency with the language of science, as well as with research protocols and processes.[7] This capacity breeds confidence and helps transform students' thinking and perceptions of themselves as scientists. Of course, such support and enablement doesn't just magically happen for students, nor does it equally ensure that all STEM students who come to college feel thusly empowered. In reality, it is the unevenness of how empowerment occurs that makes programs such as ours necessary in the first place. Underrepresented students in STEM disproportionately experience exclusion, feelings of loneliness, lack of belonging, lack of confidence, and overwhelming self-doubt.[8] The phenomenon is cyclical: being underrepresented means a student of a particular identity is not the norm in a science classroom or lab; it means the ways of being, of learning, are not often encountered enough in these spaces; it means that those who mentor, teach, design, and assess in the science space do not often share similar identities to underrepresented students. And because this is the case in many institutions, nothing much really changes over time. The culture of science continues to be dominated by a white, male sensibility[9,10]—even if led by a woman.

Our program, and many others like it, understands this phenomenon. We recognize the disruption to the science identities of students who do not seamlessly fit into the majority culture of the science space. Indeed, we actively encourage our students to create their own science "counterspace." In some ways, this is similar to the DIY science counterculture movement that seeks to democratize science, making it accessible to all[11] (in a physical sense) such as Counter Culture Labs or Garage Biology. To push back similarly against the homogeneity of mainstream science culture, STEM AP participants create a community that represents their diversity and the growing diversity of approaches to STEM. They create a community that looks like them, that embraces their diverse cultures, that honors their sexual orientations, treating all as valid components of what students can and should bring to their STEM educational experience—and later, to their professional lives. This STEM counterspace encourages its members to understand that their unique life experiences are crucial components of their STEM identity.

Reflection, Reflection, and More Reflection

One of the more powerful approaches to engaging students in developing their STEM identities involves inviting them to reflect.[12] In STEM AP, our students engage in a reflection exercise every week. At times, we provide prompts to focus their attention on particular challenges or successes, but more often, we simply ask them to reflect on anything they wish to share. Reflecting helps students make connections, understand their successes and failures, and become aware of their own learning. Reflections, meanwhile, also help teachers identify where different students are in their learning process, to gauge the success of an activity, or to simply keep track of a student's thoughts. We consider the process of reflecting to be one of our most powerful tools in helping students understand themselves and the unique abilities they can contribute to STEM. It should not escape your notice that this tool is free; its successful use in building a solid STEM identity requires only that your students engage in this activity routinely and that they trust that you are reading their most intimate thoughts with respect and with the goal of helping them learn more about themselves.

Nia is an African-American female student who came to UMass Amherst from Texas as a freshman pre-med student majoring in biology. From the moment she arrived on campus, she was scared that she would not fit in. She doubted that she had what it took to shine as a science student. She was especially apprehensive that she would not make friends very readily and would suffer isolation in her major. She immediately noted the stark difference of the western Massachusetts culture to that of her familiar hometown. At this university, she was almost anonymous. People didn't look her in the eye but passed by without acknowledging her presence.

Most of her freshman classes were held in huge lecture halls, which did not help her feelings of bewilderment. She was simply not sure she had made the right decision to come to UMass—until she joined STEM AP. She enrolled in a STEM AP Course-Based Undergraduate Research Experience (CURE), and that was the beginning of a new experience of understanding and seeing herself as a scientist. "That CURE class most importantly taught me how to be a scientist. It gave me an opportunity, as an underrepresented college student, to be seen and heard and cared for," declared Nia.

Speaking of her time as a member of STEM AP, Nia is effusive. "We are not just numbers on a sheet to them. We are people and they go out of their way to know all of us and to create a community where we help each other and share information and knowledge," she said. In her time on campus, Nia's growing confidence from being a member of our STEM AP community has pushed her to become involved with and even lead some student organizations, something she's very proud of. In her reflections, she speaks repeatedly of being inspired by the fact that among her new community of scientists, she found "people who look like me!"

Jing-mei is a shy Asian student who joined STEM AP as a freshman. She was happy she did, for she was sure she would not have made any friends on this huge campus otherwise. Jing-mei reported that attending STEM AP Monday night seminars gave her the much-needed chance to talk to people—something she might never have done had she not become a member of this community of scientists.

At the end of her second semester, Jing-mei was given the opportunity to take part in a STEM AP Summer REU, which she claims "opened a new path in my life." Jing-mei blossomed in her lab; she was also able to develop an even closer bond with her peers who had also won summer REU placements through STEM AP. Since her internship, we have watched Jing-mei grow in confidence and become even more engaged with the program. She has chosen to give back to the community by serving for two semesters as a middle school mentor. Mentoring boosted this young scholar's confidence and helped her refine her STEM identity. The opportunity to guide and explain science to her young mentees increased her certainty that she could not only understand and produce the work of science but that she was actually quite good at communicating it as well. As Jing-mei put it, "Without STEM AP, I couldn't be who I am today!"

Jing-mei's experiences are what we want *all* students to experience. We want them to come into a critical understanding about themselves as both people and professionals. They need to question the importance of their being present in a space and realize that not all of their teachers or peers see them the way we do—but what matters is how they respond and cope with this.

Many of our students have had to overcome tremendous challenges to get where they are. That resilience is something we capitalize on in STEM AP. During several of our evening sessions, we provide a forum for students to talk with each other about their personal and family journeys. These sessions are usually rich and moving, and our students often surprise themselves as they realize how far they have come and how much their families have sacrificed on their behalf. In this way, our program helps our students see that they have much to offer the field of science, and the world, in general. We help our students recognize that just as their life stories are filled with challenges, setbacks, and comebacks, science is also about trial and error. It's about the exercise of patience, perseverance, and problem-solving; it's about trying and trying again, and these are all things they are already good at. We attempt to help our students realize both that, and the reality of their own brilliance. Our students are so good at exercising patience and persistence, in fact, others could learn a great deal from them about these characteristics. But the unfamiliar science lab or classroom space makes them doubt whether they belong.

Unquestionably, they do!

STEM AP makes it clear to students that their personal journey is an *asset*. The ability to falter and survive is a person's greatest gift and strength. Students who identify as an underrepresented minority (URM) in STEM are those who know what it is to have the odds stacked against them. We help them acknowledge the extent to which they have prevailed already in their lives. Many have come from school environments that tested them to their very limit, where they encountered teachers who may have doubted their abilities and their determination to do well. By the time most of these students get to college, they have overcome tremendous odds. That is part of the precious resources they take with them to college. Yet, all too often, this is a resource they don't think of as valuable.

Annette is a first-year student who seems unusually confident, but even she had to face tough weeks that made her doubt her own mettle. Yet, her inherent resilience, which we try to help our students to harness and hone, led her to declare: "These past couple of weeks have been by far the most challenging weeks here at UMass. There have been quite a few 'lows' that have led me to question my decision to join UMass, and whether this was the best choice for me, considering my background and the kind of academic environment I am used to being [sic] around. As I reflect back on this week, I cannot help but think of the one word that kept me moving forward during these tough moments: purpose. I have decided to dedicate my next few months to search for my purpose, what truly inspired me to choose the path I have chosen for myself and what I plan to do with it. Being a part of STEM AP is truly a blessing. STEM AP provides us with many opportunities and resources that can really help us guide ourselves in this rigorous field. That being said, it can also be very intimidating and overwhelming to be around other people who seem to have everything figured out and done for their future. It is both inspiring and intimidating…"

As previously noted, we encourage our students to be reflective and self-reflexive about their chosen path and how they decide to navigate it. Doing so can equip them to remain grounded and truthful about where they are on their journey so they may regroup when necessary. Annette did so by realizing that she needed to have "purpose." In her mind, "purpose" is what would get her back on track despite feeling intimidated by peers who appeared to have everything figured out and who were well on their way to success.

We hasten to point out that helping students reach that place of re-centering or recalibrating—where they can get their bearings during the most challenging times—is one of the goals of STEM AP. We are able to achieve this by offering as well-rounded a program as possible during our Monday night seminars, which are really community meetings wherein the entire body of students comes together to learn, share, and become more familiar with each other in their own space. This learning is not limited to science or to science experiences; the engagement encompasses a wide cross-section of issues of relevance to society, and thus to their lives.

Raphael, an uncertain freshman who identifies as a first generation college student, explained it best: "STEM AP this week included a Black History Month lesson and a fun game of Kahoot. It was great to get a refresher on the background of Black History Month and why it is important. After the presentation, I felt even more aware and empowered because of it. The people before my time sacrificed and were fearless about equal treatment, so it is always good to reflect on that. Not only was Kahoot informational, but it was also fun playing with the other students of STEM AP because, since I am a new member, I am still getting to know everyone. The game made me feel even more comfortable within the STEM AP setting so I would say I am developing. It is fantastic that we not only discuss things regarding STEM but real issues that deserve attention or recognition."

As Raphael rightly noted, engaging with his peers around issues of social pertinence left him with an overall sense of connection and empowerment. It helped him and the others link their science world, often so isolating, competitive, and exclusive, to the real world issues happening seemingly outside science. It helped them make sense of their aspirations in college and beyond. As we have discussed, a student's science sense and science identity develop from being acknowledged within the science world as having the skills and aptitude to excel in it by those whom the said science world sanctions and esteems. But it also develops from a student's evolving ability to make meaning of their struggles and to see the opportunity for growth in each challenge encountered.

We are tremendously heartened each time a student arrives at the truth behind their participation in our program. As Lisa reflected: "A STEM-related activity that contributed to my personal STEM development was going to STEM AP and physically writing out the goals that I want to achieve this semester. Writing my goals down made me see them clearly for the first time and motivated me to keep working hard so that I can achieve them."

Designing a Program to Foster Personal Growth

It is also reassuring to hear that our students see purpose in the way we designed our program. Jenna certainly seemed to understand our intent in this regard, even to the extent of acknowledging the need to give back to a community that had given her so much: "STEM was very enjoyable this week as I found myself immersed within my community. The Monday night seminar was incredibly enjoyable as it was primarily student [led]. I think it is important that we incorporate culturally relevant presentations within the cycle of our nightly activities. I also enjoyed attending our weekly meeting for middle school mentoring, as I got to speak with Ethan and others regarding the future of the program. I hope that I can continue to enjoy the spoils of this community; hopefully, one day, I may give back to the community through which I have excelled and prospered."

Josie, a sophomore, also found the Black History Month presentation to be very useful in reinforcing her STEM identity: "This past week in STEM AP, we started the seminar with a presentation from the UMass chapter of the Black Student Union (BSU). It was inspiring to hear all about the hard work the students do as part of the BSU to spread education about the history of advancement of African-Americans. It reminded me of one of the many reasons I love being in STEM AP: it is a program that aims to aid in the advancement of underrepresented students in STEM. After the Kahoot game, where I learned a lot of fun trivia about famous African-American individuals, we split into class-level programming where we worked on our resumes. My resume was already complete, or so I thought, and through peer review, I found a couple of grammatical errors in my resume. We also discussed CVs, and after the program, I went back to my dorm and started to draft my own CV."

We have been deliberate in our design of the STEM AP. The program works best when it is collaborative and co-creative—when we hear from students and are able to respond to their needs as issues arise. As has been previously affirmed, we encourage active participation by building a community, a counterspace that makes it easier for students to so engage. The support they get as students who identify as first generation college students, Pell Grant eligible, which indicates a more precarious or lower socioeconomic position for the household, or students of color, is absolutely necessary because most of their professors or graduate mentors are not people who either look like them or share their experiences. We understand how profoundly limiting the experience of a college science classroom can be for our students. Again, this is not because they, in any way, lack the requisite creativity or intellectual heft to excel, but because they feel out of sorts, out of place, and outside of what is considered normative for the insiders. As outsiders, they are disproportionately assumed to be incapable of success as STEM scholars. They must, therefore, fight on several levels: to overcome the natural increased difficulty of college-level work; to get acquainted with the college experience, including living on a college campus with newfound independence; to find new friends and communities; and to cope with the deficit assumptions of professors and teaching assistants, and with having to persist in spite of them.

Our students have the extraordinary privilege of regularly participating in community-building exercises during Monday night seminars and being able to visit the STEM AP office to interact with staff and students. This opportunity was of particular value to Asa, a female student of color who found herself in need of some guidance and advice after she became particularly stressed one week: "This week I went to the STEM AP office to talk with Sonji about personal issues, school-related stress, and if I wanted to continue to apply to more REUs. After some open conversation about my mental and emotional drain and fatigue, Sonji suggested that I do what's best for my well-being by prioritizing what mattered to me. Being able to talk to Sonji at the STEM AP office and knowing that I have mentors to go to within the STEM field really reassures me and I'm happy I can come to them for guidance."

Building a solid community that offers stability, support, and care across as many facets of student life as possible looms large in our program. We understand at a fundamental level that the identity of being a STEM scholar is not the only identity our students carry. As a program, our enduring aspiration is to cater to the all-encompassing, all-inclusive identity of the human being and all of what it means in the experiences of our varied students. This is exactly the juncture where we want students to meet each other: at the table of inclusion and equity. As students become more familiar with each other, they come to see more in each other that reveals how much they have in common—and *that* is the stuff that community is made of.

This is exactly what Andy, a male Caucasian who identifies as a first generation college student and Pell Grant eligible, discovered: "This week has been a week in which I certainly improved my STEM identity and actively participated in very beneficial events. It all started with my Monday night STEM AP seminar, where we all sat down with a group and learned more about each other through fun ice-breakers, something that made me get to know my fellow scholars better. After that, we had an informative and entertaining presentation by Ethan about studying abroad, when he shared his wonderful experience of studying in Barcelona. I am sure it was an eye-opening event for many people and must have made some people consider studying abroad more. My next STEM experience this week was with middle school mentoring on Wednesday, when I helped the kids in my group design a water filter that would filter out dirt, rocks, and other serious water contaminants. This helped develop the kids' STEM identities, as they learned about global water pollution and how a simple water filter works. In addition, I developed my character."

Andy "developed his character"—how fundamental and important is that self-proclamation! He did so through engaging in community building and by mentoring younger students. This is a powerful accomplishment. Developing a science identity is absolutely about shaping and developing the characters of the students we serve. It creates a fundamental change in students' perception of the world and how they view themselves going forward and, not insignificantly, how they view and relate to others inside and outside the science space. This is not something that we expressly promote as a benefit of joining our program, but as we witness the awakening that takes place in our students, we see a change that overtakes them. They become more confident scientists who learn the language, knowledge, and skills of science—but at the same time, they also learn how to impart this knowledge to their juniors, how to share their knowledge with peers and with mentors and instructors, and how to engage with and expect to engage with scientists of varying backgrounds and experiences.

We watch with fascination as our students put themselves forward in the competitive science sphere, as Lauren did when she attended a career fair: "This past week, I went to the engineering career fair. The only reason I had the confidence to go was because of what I learned at STEM AP. I completely remade my resume and I looked into some of the companies so I felt prepared for the fair. I don't know if I [will] get an internship out of it, but it was a very valuable opportunity and introduction to work life."

Helping the students we serve develop a STEM identity also means helping them accept themselves wholly, despite the whiteness and maleness of most science spaces. We attempt to fortify our students' sense of self and self-understanding in a way that will allow them to hold their own in an environment that does not necessarily honor who they are.

A Surprising, Unexpected Benefit

The power of this transformation in our students' sense of self as scientists revealed itself fairly early in the development of STEM AP, and in an unexpected way. Prof. Riley runs a research laboratory at UMass and hosts 15 undergraduate researchers at any time, 50% of which are STEM AP students. She observed that the STEM AP students often possessed characteristics lacking in many of the non-STEM AP students. First, they enter the lab with a level of self-confidence far beyond their ages and grade levels. They appear far more relaxed in lab meetings and less anxious about how to "fit in" to the lab culture. Most students arrive in a new lab hesitant, anxious about what they don't know, fearful of saying something wrong. In contrast, the STEM AP students arrive self-confident, excited to be there and ready to dive in.

Second, they are more adept at working in teams. Students often come to lab with a sense that they are going to individually solve some problem or make some great discovery. This is a perspective cultivated in many labs and promulgated through the media, and it is one that students often try to emulate on arrival. We call it the alpha male scientist syndrome. For many years, the alpha male syndrome permeated the culture of the Riley lab, too. After all, it was how she was trained to engage in science: individuals fiercely compete as they race to find the answer. As more STEM AP students joined the lab, however, they contributed to creating a new culture, one that resulted in a lab that now *only* engages in team-based research. There are no individuals working on their own any longer—everyone belongs to a team. This often creates discomfort for non-STEM AP students, who feel the need to prove themselves as individuals and may have a difficult time adapting to a team environment. Not so for the STEM AP students—they relish teamwork.

The primary difference between the STEM AP and non-STEM AP students in Prof. Riley's lab, lies in the fact that the former students spend their first year at college working with graduate and peer mentors; many take a CURE, and all spend time developing their STEM identities in the STEM AP seminar program. In contrast, while the non-STEM AP students have generally taken a course with Prof. Riley, they are not involved in any of the training and mentoring experiences provided by STEM AP. Although the sample sizes are small, it appears to Prof. Riley that one year in STEM AP results in a profound transformation in students, producing young scholars with a far stronger sense of themselves as scientists, an increased self-confidence, and a greater ease in engaging in teamwork.

This is not an insignificant point: in order to help our students become okay with who they are and what they know or don't know, they have to learn to be comfortable in STEM spaces, such as research labs, to the point of celebrating themselves. Prof. Riley watched as the STEM AP students transformed her lab community into one in which students were more team oriented, more willing to help each other, and generally more comfortable. She watched as her lab become a more enjoyable place for students to gain research experience. The students smiled more often and spent more time studying together or just hanging out in the student office areas. Her lab transformed from one in which individuals were the focus into one in which research teams were the main source of productivity and success. Thus, STEM AP's sense of community not only transforms students, it transforms spaces as well as professors if they care to be self-reflexive.

URM students may believe, at the outset, that they have nothing to add to the science space. Many may not yet have developed the skills or the language to easily navigate the STEM arena as it exists in most places. But by being made to make meaning of their own experiences and perspectives, they undergo a perception change. It is one that empowers them and allows them to engage in science in an entirely different way. STEM AP students appear to relish their teams at a level Prof. Riley has not seen in most other students. Perhaps this is because they come from a strong community in STEM AP, a community that provides the support they require to be comfortable bringing themselves to the table. Prof. Riley notes that, "Regardless of the underlying reason, these students bring a sense of joy to engaging in science that I have not experienced in over 30 years of research!"

References

1. Renninger, K. A. Interest and Identity Development in Instruction: An Inductive Model. *Educ. Psychol.* **2009**, *44* (2), 105–118. DOI:10.1080/00461520902832392.
2. Martin-Hansen, L. Examining Ways to Meaningfully Support Students in STEM. *Int. J. STEM Educ.* **2018**, *5* (1), 53. DOI:10.1186/s40594-018-0150-3.

3. Killpack, T. L.; Melón, L. C. Toward Inclusive STEM Classrooms: What Personal Role Do Faculty Play? *CBE Life Sci. Educ.* **2016**, *15* (3). DOI:10.1187/cbe.16-01-0020.
4. Rainey, K.; Dancy, M.; Mickelson, R.; Stearns, E.; Moller, S. Race and Gender Differences in How Sense of Belonging Influences Decisions to Major in STEM. *Int. J. STEM Educ.* **2018**, *5* (1), 10. DOI:10.1186/s40594-018-0115-6.
5. Ireland, D. T.; Freeman, K. E.; Winston-Proctor, C. E.; DeLaine, K. D.; McDonald Lowe, S.; Woodson, K. M. (Un)Hidden Figures: A Synthesis of Research Examining the Intersectional Experiences of Black Women and Girls in STEM Education. *Rev. Res. Educ.* **2018**, *42* (1), 226–254. DOI:10.3102/0091732X18759072.
6. González-Pérez, S.; Mateos de Cabo, R.; Sáinz, M. Girls in STEM: Is It a Female Role-Model Thing? *Front. Psychol.* **2020**, *11*, 2204. DOI:10.3389/fpsyg.2020.02204.
7. *Charting a Course for Success: America's Strategy for STEM Education. A Report by the Committee on STEM Education of the National Science & Technology Council*; ED590474; Executive Office of the White House: National Science and Technology Council, 2018; p 48.
8. Fisher, A. J.; Mendoza-Denton, R.; Patt, C.; Young, I.; Eppig, A.; Garrell, R. L.; Rees, D. C.; Nelson, T. W.; Richards, M. A. Structure and Belonging: Pathways to Success for Underrepresented Minority and Women PhD Students in STEM Fields. *PLoS One* **2019**, *14* (1), e0209279. DOI:10.1371/journal.pone.0209279.
9. Woolston, C. White Men Still Dominate in UK Academic Science. *Nature* **2020**, *579* (7800), 622–622. DOI:10.1038/d41586-020-00759-1.
10. Wood, S.; Henning, J. A.; Chen, L.; McKibben, T.; Smith, M. L.; Weber, M.; Zemenick, A.; Ballen, C. J. A Scientist Like Me: Demographic Analysis of Biology Textbooks Reveals Both Progress and Long-Term Lags. *Proc. R. Soc. B Biol. Sci.* **2020**, *287* (1929), 20200877. DOI:10.1098/rspb.2020.0877.
11. Talbot, M. Hacking the Body: The Scientific Counter-Culture of the DIYbio Movement. *New Yorker.* May 25, 2020.
12. Talafian, H.; Moy, M. K.; Woodard, M. A.; Foster, A. N. STEM Identity Exploration Through an Immersive Learning Environment. *J. STEM Educ. Res.* **2019**, *2* (2), 105–127. DOI:10.1007/s41979-019-00018-7.

Chapter 3

The Power of Mentoring

From the Very Beginning

It is a bright and sunny morning, not long after Labor Day. The skies are clear, the breeze crisp, and an undeniable aura of anticipation and excitement is in the air. You wake up in a dorm room, away from your family and loved ones, as you prepare to head out to your first day at university. Yet, as you trek across the campus to your first college lecture, a growing realization dawns upon you. This university is big... no, not just big... *very* big. The reality of attending an institution with more than 28,000 students suddenly becomes vividly clear to you. Thousands of students are shuffling along sidewalks, crossing roads, scattering in all directions around you. They may be physically close, but they feel miles away with their headphones on and thoughts centered on their paths, as you must navigate your own.

As you enter the lecture hall, you look at what will become the focus of your next four years: a massive auditorium equipped with surround sound... and 300 strangers arrayed in rows, looming over the professor's podium below. You find an empty seat and the professor begins the chemistry lecture immediately. You physically participate only once during the class by pressing a button on an iClicker remote in response to a query from the lecturer. Your iClicker registration soon becomes your primary identity in the class. As you continue to attend one large lecture after another, you begin to feel overwhelmed. As the loneliness settles in, a daunting realization surfaces: you are nothing more than a small fish navigating a vast ocean of academics and it is up to you to sink or swim.

Why Does This Matter?

These sentiments of confusion, uncertainty, fear, and loneliness are universally experienced by college students across the nation.[1] In a 2017 American College Health Association report, 63% of students surveyed reported feeling very lonely over the past 12 months.[2] Roughly half also reported feeling hopeless at times, and even more reported experiencing overwhelming anxiety. A disturbing 40% reported feeling so depressed at times that it was difficult for them to function.[2] Yet, what is even more alarming is that these statistics only worsen when we focus on first-generation college students and students of color.[3,4] In fact, research has indicated that students of color are nearly twice as likely to *not* seek professional care when they feel depressed or anxious, in comparison

Empowering Underrepresented Students in Science. DOI: http://dx.doi.org/10.1016/B978-0-323-90469-8.00003-2

to their white peers.[5,6] It's no wonder that 50% of our STEM majors either drop out of college or leave their STEM majors before they graduate.[7] Perhaps we should be amazed that half of them actually persevere!

The root of such emotions, particularly in STEM students, isn't difficult to imagine. Between intense prerequisite courses and grueling laboratory sessions, along with the highly competitive nature of many of their fellow students and the lack of connection with their instructors, the possible causes of such stress are never-ending.[8,9] First-generation college students and URM students are especially vulnerable to these stressors, not least because of weaker support networks: a missing sense of belonging, additional work-study obligation, and quite simply, the lack of added guidance and wisdom from parents and mentors who have previously navigated the halls of academia.[10,8]

These sentiments and challenges have been expressed to us by our STEM Ambassador students time and time again. Their weekly reflections are filled with them. *"I feel like a failure, so why should I even bother trying?" "What am I supposed to do with my life?" "It's not possible for someone like me." "They say I'm not smart enough." "No one's going to even consider someone like me." "I can't do everything that they're doing and still succeed." "Why should I listen to anyone? They don't understand me... no one does."*

If students are to bring their full talent, energy, motivation, and passion to their studies, it is critical that from their very first day at college, they know there is a support system in place *specifically for them*. This is true for all students, but it's particularly critical for STEM students as they perceive their academic path as being "harder" and more highly competitive.[11,12] The support offered must be personal, tailored to their particular needs, and available *before* the feelings of depression, loneliness, and anxiety set in, let alone fester.[7] Vast resources are available for students at most universities and colleges. However, our students routinely report that they didn't know about those resources, were afraid to ask for help, didn't want others to know about their fears, or simply didn't think they had time to deal with their emotions.

While developing STEM AP, we focused intensely on creating a support system to meet the specific needs of our students. We recognized the power of mentoring,[13] particularly, peer mentoring, that is, enlisting other STEM students to help their younger peers navigate academic challenges and address their anxieties and fears.[14] We knew that we needed to create a powerful, comprehensive, supportive mentoring network for all of our students, one that would be a reassuring presence in their college life from their first days on campus through the end of their undergraduate experience. And so, we did just that.

Constructing a STEM Mentoring Network

What does it take to be a successful STEM mentor? Ask five different people and you will get five different answers. For some, a mentor is an individual they look up to, perhaps a STEM researcher or professor. For others, it is the role model they use to mold their own STEM identity: a physician, an engineer, or an astronaut. For many, it is the person who sees more promise and talent in them than they can see in themselves. And still others simply want an experienced guide to help them navigate the personal, professional, and institutional challenges they come up against.

For students of color and those from other underrepresented backgrounds, a mentor may serve as the most instrumental lifeline in building a better future for themselves.[15] Why? Because for URM students, a mentor with shared experiences embodies the reality of what it means to achieve one's goals in a world where the odds are stacked against them. Such a mentor serves as proof that no matter the color of your skin, the circumstances you were born into, or the way in which you are perceived and treated by the world, you are capable and worthy of transforming your dreams into reality.[14]

Knowing this, our program purposefully created a robust mentoring network. We engage graduate students to mentor undergraduates, encourage more advanced undergraduates to mentor their younger peers, and provide opportunity for all of our students to mentor middle school students—the youth of tomorrow. At every stage, we train our mentors and provide guidance on how to approach mentoring deliberately, employing inclusive practices. In the sections below, we describe each component of our mentoring web.

However, let us start by stating our mentoring philosophy. Our guiding principle is that each of our students has valuable resources that they bring to the STEM space; specifically, those very resources and ideas that are unique, powerful, and perhaps even transformative, to the world of STEM. This may seem like a strange thing to have to state—"we value all comers"—but for those of us inside the walls of STEM education, we know that many of the very earliest courses in a STEM major are specifically designed to ensure that a large fraction of students fail. Rather than view this outcome as a failure of the instructor, it is accepted as the necessary cost of "weeding out" those not meant for the rigors of STEM studies. This outrageous and unacceptable perspective should be the focus of another book, but for now, we will accept that for some STEM instructors, it is simply a fact.

While the importance of providing every student with a mentor cannot be overstated, it is the relationship itself that will determine the success of this interaction. Studies of mentoring relationships have pointed to three key factors in predicting a positive outcome: psychosocial support, relationship satisfaction (including levels of trust, respect, and empathy) and instrumental support in the form of resources and opportunities.[16,17] Like all relationships, an impactful mentoring relationship demands quality time, energy, knowledge, and mutual understanding between the mentor and mentee. With special regard for these factors, we set out to establish an interconnected mentoring web involving each and every one of our STEM AP students.

Graduate Student Mentors Share Their Wisdom and Experience

As soon as our first-year students arrive on campus, they are paired with a graduate mentor. These mentors play a vital role in helping our students integrate into their majors and our program. The mentors offer a depth and breadth of shared experiences that help to inspire and guide the paths of our budding STEM AP scholars. Each graduate mentor is assigned three or four undergraduates with the mission of connecting personally to them, while providing support as they develop their research, academic, and social skills. The critical need to proactively provide URM students with graduate mentors who can connect with them on the most personal levels cannot be overstated.

"I was at first apprehensive joining a PWI [Primarily White Institution]. Before college started, I didn't know if I would be welcomed or who I could really look up to for advice," said Jayla, a STEM AP student majoring in Biomedical Engineering. "But then, the first day I arrived at STEM AP, I saw a community that was truly ready to accept me with open arms for who I was. I love this program a lot and while it gave me more than I ever anticipated, it also opened up opportunities for me to serve others in ways I never imagined."

Jayla, an African-American woman of Haitian descent from the northeast, is the youngest of her siblings and the first in her family to attend college. As a Black woman, first-generation college student, and Pell Grant recipient, she joined STEM AP looking for both community and mentorship in her field of engineering—a field notorious for its lack of women, let alone women of color. "I still remember first being told I was assigned to a graduate mentor from engineering," she said. "I had an image of what the person would look like, and then in walked Eva... And I can't even begin to talk about STEM AP's impact on me without mentioning her. For the first time, I was seeing a woman who had gone to state school, studied hard, and was currently getting her PhD in Transportation Engineering. Even though it was a different field of engineering than mine, it was her mentorship that has had the most profound impact on my career goals, more so than any other mentor I've ever had."

Similar to all of our graduate mentorships, Jayla's experience began with learning how to read and interpret articles from the primary literature in her mentor's field. But it didn't end there. "Eva took us to her engineering lab, which was incredible and had this life-size built-in car. She taught us how to work the simulator and the mechanisms of the gas, brakes, wheel rotations and their signals, and how they all worked in sync with each other. It was so amazing to look at from the inside! This was my first tour of an engineering lab and it really changed what I envisioned an engineer to be and where I saw a future for myself."

Time and again, we hear from our students about the importance of having a graduate mentor. Adam, a shy first-year student who rarely opened up in his reflections, nonetheless made special mention of his graduate mentors. "This week, I want to highlight what I did with my graduate mentors Carey and Adrian. They taught me and the other members of my group to read research papers and grasp the knowledge of how to do so. Personally, I want to get into a lab in the spring to do research, so my mentors asked whose lab I want to be a part of and then had me read papers that were from the primary investigator (PI) in that lab. This way, when I speak with the PI in the future, I will have talking points. I found this week very helpful and the guidance from my mentors very useful."

Our graduate mentors possess a myriad of lab experiences and actively participate in bench or field research. They offer STEM AP students like Jayla and Adam an in-depth exploration of STEM fields while challenging the outdated stereotypes of what it looks like to be a scientist. Due to their shared life experiences, our mentors know what it feels like to be scared, lonely, and uncertain, as well as the constant stress to outperform their peers, an unspoken necessity for many URM students. We capitalize on these shared experiences and build our graduate mentor training based not only upon what a mentor has to offer an undergraduate in terms of their knowledge and experience, but upon what a mentor will learn from their mentee and from the mentoring experience in general.

We initially framed our graduate mentor training program around the methods detailed in the well-known and highly effective STEM mentor training manual, *Entering Mentoring*.[18] However, we soon realized that for our mentors to help guide their mentees in the process of developing their own STEM identity, they, too, needed to reflect on their own sense of self as STEM researchers. We began to implement a new mentoring model, which we call AMR: Affinity, Mutuality, Reciprocity. **Affinity** speaks to the sense of connection and affection that the mentor will develop with the mentee—an affection that will inspire trust and mutual caring. **Mutuality** suggests a sense of mutual respect and engagement that marks the relationship and allows for full mentee and mentor buy-in. **Reciprocity** highlights that the mentoring relationship is important to both the mentor and the mentee: both sides derive purpose and value from being a part of this relationship. Thus, the AMR model has a philosophical underpinning that honors the life experiences of both the mentee and mentor and which understands that each side will bring different things to the relationship, but that these different contributions are of equal value. We impress upon our mentors that their approach to their mentees must never be from a deficit perspective, in which mentees are deemed to have little to bring to the table, but rather to honor the challenges both sides have already overcome to be present today. Why? Because we recognize the wealth of the experiences these students bring to our program and consider it essential that our mentors encourage their mentees to appreciate the power that their personal experiences give to the process of developing their own STEM identities.

Our mentor training program is based on an apprenticeship model. Graduate mentors are trained on a particular skill or activity one week and then put that skill to use in their mentoring meetings the very next week. Mentors report feeling prepared and confident in their mentoring, ready to engage their students and to guide them in a determined manner. This training takes place over the course of a semester. The result is a team of skilled mentors who are ready to help mentees perceive and ultimately utilize the immeasurable value of their life experiences while shepherding them through activities to hone their research skills.

"Even to this day, I'm still in touch with my graduate mentor, Emma," said Eliza, a STEM AP student who immigrated from Israel and undertook a double major in Biochemistry and Spanish. "The graduate mentor program was my favorite part of STEM AP. Unlike most mentors I've had, Emma really challenged me to reflect on why I wanted to do the things I did and what was truly important in order for me to get there. She was such a unique person because she had a family of her own, with children, and was then pursuing graduate school in her late 30s. She had planned to go to medical school years ago, was accepted, but was so passionate about research that she didn't go... And that was really important for me to hear, because I learned that it was okay to embrace change and that life didn't always happen in a straight line. [...] And she cared so much about us, because we'd have many conversations outside of the program where she not only gave me advice but would really listen to me and make me feel valued. [...] She didn't just challenge me to think deeper about my own life experiences but pushed me to use those experiences in creating the kind of female scientist I'd hope to become."

These are the kinds of stories we hear time and again from our STEM AP graduate mentees. Whether igniting a passion for STEM or challenging students to reflect and cherish their life experiences while learning to believe in themselves, our graduate mentorship program has had a profound impact in shaping the perspectives and career ambitions of many of our STEM AP students.

In large part, the willingness and responsiveness of our graduate mentors are born of the caliber of mentors recruited to our program, but it is also due to the thoughtful and structured training that they receive. The issues of salience to our STEM Ambassador participants are brought to the fore of the graduate mentor trainings. In other words, the STEM AP graduate mentor training makes visible the usually invisible issues that hold URM students back from performing to the fullest of their potential. Our training activates an acute awareness of the inequities that lurk under the surface of science learning spaces and which account for many of the difficulties students such as ours face as they try to navigate their way through college.

Near-Peer Mentors Connect Most Closely With Their Mentees

In addition to their graduate student mentors, STEM AP participants are also provided with a near-peer mentor. First-year students are paired with fourth-year mentors, while second-year students are mentored by third-year students. Third- and fourth-year students are uniquely positioned to support their younger peers. They have experienced similar academic and social pressures and have had time to reflect on who they are, develop a more robust STEM identity, and gain a more nuanced perspective on what they want from their academic experiences. These near peers bring this knowledge and experience to their mentoring relationships as they provide critical guidance and support. This close mentoring relationship is a powerful way for our program to take the pulse of our younger students, ensuring that they are not slipping through the cracks or struggling with challenges they have not yet chosen to share.

"I still remember my peer mentor, Shonda. She was such an awesome person! I am not really the talkative kind of person, I'd say, and I had found it really hard getting myself into social situations," recalled Ediye, a first-generation college student and recent transfer from a local community college who originally emigrated from Nigeria. "I was so nervous about college, and so when we came to the first Monday session, I was like, 'Ahh, I don't know if I want to do this' in my head. But then Shonda walked up to me and [said], 'Okay, so today we're going to start talking about school and programs and difficulties that we're facing in class.' And then after that, she'd ask us what the next step was in our challenges and what we'd do about it. She really played a very big part in making me speak up and into who I am now. STEM AP was the best decision I'd say I made at UMass Amherst, because before that time, I was feeling really left out; nothing felt good because I just went to school and then back to my dorm every day… but then thanks to the people I met at STEM AP, I got really comfortable and felt welcomed! We met each other every week to have dinner and also got to talk about our transfer issues and how we've been coping and stuff like that."

For all students majoring in STEM, navigating the undergraduate years can be an isolating and lonely experience. For students of color and first-generation college students, however, these challenges are even greater. It is for this precise reason we strive to build an inclusive community that acknowledges and responds to the emotions and struggles of our students, employing role models with shared experiences. "When I see the other amazing mentors from STEM AP, I'm like, 'I don't want to be that kid who is not doing well when everyone else is doing well.' So now you actually know those people, and it's not just having amazing students at STEM AP, who show you how much you know even though it's not easy… It's the reminder I'm still doing it, you know, and I'm not giving up on all that. […] And this gave me this confidence and motivation that I can do it, no matter how hard it is," shared Ediye.

Unlike their peers from more privileged families, many of our STEM AP students face additional challenges outside their STEM studies. Whether searching for acceptance or a sense of belonging or negotiating the challenges of balancing their STEM courses with working multiple campus jobs to make ends meet, our students crave mentors who truly understand their lives, having navigated similar paths. In fact, it is for these reasons that STEM AP's near-peer mentoring program quickly became one of most beloved and talked-about mentoring programs on campus. As STEM AP students shared their experiences outside our walls, they, in turn, helped to engage their friends and peers, thus expanding the program to become the richly diverse and inclusive network we have today.

"I still remember when STEM AP first started, it was about 20 of us students in a small classroom, excited to get to know one another... And then before we knew it, there were over 100 students in the program!" exclaimed Amira, a recent STEM AP graduate who majored in Biochemistry and Molecular Biology. "Near-peer mentoring was one of my most favorite parts of STEM AP and it made me believe anything was possible," she said. "I trusted my mentor so much and felt more comfortable asking her questions than I would've felt asking my closest friends or advisors. It felt like having a guide to navigate the tougher parts of life and for that, I am incredibly grateful. At the time I started STEM AP, I had just immigrated from Lebanon and was struggling to find my identity. I was so shy and just terrified of everything and I barely knew what I wanted to do with my life either... But what I didn't realize was how hard it is to envision a path for yourself when you don't understand who you are or what you want in life. That's where STEM AP and mentoring came in. And everything took off from there... I learned to develop confidence and to take initiative, and to *not* be intimidated by life. STEM AP gave me the courage to stand up for myself and that made all the difference."

As a shy, young Middle Eastern woman navigating college in a new country, Amira had joined STEM AP with a severe lack of self-confidence and an overwhelming fear of public speaking. But it was her brilliant mind, kind nature, and resilience that took her far. Over her four years in STEM AP, she quickly grew into one of our most inspiring near-peer mentors and most effective leaders, ultimately giving talks in front of hundreds of students and becoming the STEM AP undergraduate program manager by her senior year.

"I think near-peer mentoring is so important to this program because we are the ones who know what it's like for one another," said Amira. "When you are underrepresented in a community, you are in the minority. And you will always feel like you have a smaller voice than everybody else. That's not because it's true, but because that's how society makes you feel and that's how it's always been. I used to think that maybe it was because I had an accent or because I don't speak the same as those around me... that I don't share their experiences and I'm not from here, so I won't be accepted or heard. [...] But what I learned in STEM AP is that you have to accept yourself first, before anyone around you does. And then you need to articulate your thoughts and speak with conviction, and that's what makes someone heard."

Over the course of her undergraduate years, Amira went on to develop a passion for neuropsychology research while becoming heavily involved in her campus community. Immediately after graduating, she went on to become a clinical research assistant, after which she was recruited by a distinguished research scientist at Harvard Medical School to join his inaugural Center for Brain Circuit Therapeutics.

The skills that Amira discusses are at the core of our near-peer mentoring experience. During the initial months of STEM AP, near-peer mentors and their mentees are simply tasked with getting to know one another. This occurs first through a series of queries about academic interests, hobbies, and career goals and then through diving deeper into their past experiences and sense of self. These discussions play a critical role in establishing trust and strengthening the mentoring relationship. Over the course of the year, mentors build a proactive dialogue with their mentees in an effort to guide them into thinking critically about themselves: Who am I? Do I belong? Why do I belong? Will I make it? Others don't believe in me, why should I believe in myself? These are just a few of the many questions our students are invited to address over the course of their first year.

"STEM AP really taught me how to talk freely and build those communication skills… I watched how my mentors took care of me and I learned to treat my mentees the same way," said Dara, a first-generation college student and immigrant from West Africa. "Through STEM AP, I had two mentees, one who was in the Physics Department and the other in Computer Science. The peer mentoring helped me a lot, even just to learn more about those around me. My mentees were immigrants from India, and I actually got to find out so many similarities that Indians have with Nigerians. We talked about our cultures and experiences and it was just amazing to hear how much we had in common. And so, even though there were a lot of differences, I still feel like I got to know about what this new country and culture were like. My Physics mentee was also a first-generation student who was having problems choosing his major. I told him my own story because I too had struggled with my major and had struggled to find out where I was supposed to be. I told him that if he's not doing well and he wants to do something more or different, he should look at his hobbies and his values… really look at what it is you like to do and then see how you can build a career in that particular direction. […] And it worked out really, really well for him."

Dara's mentoring experience highlights a core message of our STEM AP mentorship program: There is more that connects us than that which sets us apart. Her resiliency, patience, and ability to deeply care for her mentees directly impacted their undergraduate experiences in meaningful ways. "I especially liked helping first-generation college students because it really is their first time experiencing college, for themselves and their families," she mused. "I think that's why they find it very difficult to understand different college things and which direction to take. I have been there and I think it's important to talk to someone who can understand you and guide you on what path to take. STEM Ambassadors taught me that even if you try something and you fail, you still have the ability to excel at it later on… For me, giving up was not an option anymore. And in so many ways, if I look back, I know that I have given up a lot in my life; like, *really* a lot. But then with my experiences in STEM AP, I decided that I'm not going to give up anymore, and that even when I feel like I'm failing, I'll still try. [...] I've learned to never lose hope, that things will get better, and to share this message with others around me."

A staple of our near-peer mentoring program is a brief series of round-table questions that occur every other week at the start of the class-level programming session. These questions often start with a casual tone, centering on each other's lives at the moment. For example, students are asked: *How did you spend your weekend? What was your favorite part of today? What are you looking forward to tomorrow?* As the mentees take turns engaging in conversations with their mentor and fellow mentees, the round-table concludes with the most personal question of the day. The goal here is to guide our younger students into reflecting upon their lives and sharing those experiences that lie at the core of who they are in order to build and strengthen their bonds with their mentor. To delve into this discussion, we ask questions such as: *What was the most difficult experience you've ever had in your life? When you look to the future, what are you most afraid of? When you think of your family, what do they mean to you? Has anyone in your life doubted your ability to succeed? If so, how did it make you feel and how would you respond to it today? When you think about the hardest moments in your life, what gave you the strength to persevere?*

At first glance, these questions appear rather invasive and extremely personal—more than most peer mentorships would dare to address. And yet, while our students are never compelled to share any information they do not wish to, nearly all of them willingly open up about their experiences, often to their own surprise. Why do our students choose to share their most intimate thoughts and experiences? We believe this openness is due to their acknowledgement of the accepting, supportive community that is STEM AP. From the moment they join our program, we stand with open arms, inviting each student in and acknowledging them as unique, talented individuals with limitless possibilities ahead of them. We unconditionally embrace every student who steps forward.

"Freshman year was one of my hardest years of college. I came in with the expectation that it would be fairly easy since classes, most of them being 100 level, were rumored to be easy; that's all I heard. Instead, I found myself crying every night and didn't make any new friends... I went through my first year of college alone [...] My mother never went to college, barely even finishing high school and I (being the oldest of my siblings) was the first in my household to attend. This caused me to struggle so much because I didn't even have the help at home since no one could relate or understand," recalled Leah, a sophomore Biology major who identifies as a Black woman and first-generation college student. "But then, I enrolled in STEM AP and from that moment on, college was a life-changing experience. I no longer felt the need to cry every night because I knew that I wasn't alone. STEM peer mentorship is like the classroom version of a Yellow Book. They have so much useful information and resources for students and have created a community that has felt more like a family...

It is very difficult being first generation because without the support and motivation, it is quite hard to move forward [...] I was once a caterpillar, struggling to get past the larva stage, and for me, STEM has guided me into metamorphosis. [...] And I really wish that everyone who is underrepresented in college could experience this."

Many of our students have dealt with more trauma and heartache than their more advantaged peers can imagine. They have shared stories about their experiences of exclusion and of feeling their difference in the academic space. They have talked of navigating the death of parents or losing siblings at a young age due to violence. They have opened up about childhoods spent in foster care and growing up in a world where they never felt wanted. They have conveyed what it felt like to be homeless or go hungry when their families couldn't make ends meet. They've even shared the vivid fears and heartache of leaving behind one's entire life in order to escape a war-torn country they once called home.

And then there were the conversations of hope and promise. Students shared their inspiring desire to work hard and give themselves and their families a better life than they were afforded. They embodied and articulated the strength to dream and move with determination toward careers they were told they'd never achieve. And lastly, they told their peers about their unwavering belief that they are in charge of their own destiny and can chart their path as they wish it to be.

Having experienced similar challenges, near-peer mentors often relate more closely to our younger students than any other advisors, instructors, or mentors. These shared experiences allow deep and healing conversations about those challenging memories that so drastically impact a student's identity and self-worth. The mentoring sessions foster a sense of promise and optimism as our students experience the acceptance and reassurance offered by an older student who has traveled some of the same paths and succeeded. This process of sharing and acknowledging past challenges is key to ensuring our students become integrated into the STEM AP community and are able to—and indeed crave to—work toward building their professional and social identities.

"One of the mentors who really stood out to me was my own mentor, Jasmine, who recently graduated. As my mentor, she really helped me to be more comfortable reaching out to both faculty and my advisors," reflected Ruby, a Black woman and first-generation college student majoring in Biology. "During both my time while being mentored by her and prior, I actually had a really bad relationship with my advisors... There were just many times where I felt like we didn't click and that I wasn't being heard. My mentoring experience [with Jasmine] really helped me to *not* generalize all advisors and make assumptions on the kind of support I would receive. [...] She showed us the amazing relationship that she had with a different advisor, and given how highly they spoke of each other, it really helped open my eyes to the possibilities of just knowing that there really are people rooting for you," stated Ruby. "And as for Jasmine, just by meeting another student who is also first generation and a woman of color looking to be a leader in her field, that was very inspiring to me. [...]

I loved how we were able to vent to each other and also have various perspectives about how things went. [...] Just by really being able to unpack it and share our experiences, I felt like it was a really great way to connect with someone that I wouldn't have otherwise met. [...] It forced me into a position to really deliver things with thought and to act with purpose. I am now in a position where I have to internalize and reflect on all of the positions and experiences that I've had and pass it on to someone else who could really use the valuable information I had. In a lot of ways, it also helped me gain confidence in myself looking back at all that I've been through. A lot of times in certain headspace when things aren't going right, I often feel like my own worst critic. But being in a position from where I can see what all I've been through and what I've actually gained from that, to the point that someone else is actually seeking it from me, it's honestly just very nice, to put it simply."

The vast wealth of knowledge and campus experiences our near-peer mentors bring to the table can ultimately ease the transition of our first- and second-year students into campus life. Year after year, we see many of our students enter the program as shy and introverted, often lacking self-confidence, with no sense of belonging. And by the time they are upperclassmen, they are transformed.

"I remember I was a Biology major talking about STEM with my near-peer mentor who was studying Environmental Sciences," said Santiago, a STEM AP sophomore brought up in a traditional Columbian household. "And then, the conversation flipped to extracurriculars and he saw that I had an interest in our student government association [SGA] but had never approached them. [...] I still remember that day, because the very next thing he did was pull out his SGA contact card and wrote down their contact info on my paper. He said, 'You'd be great at this and you just let me know if you're ready, because I'll put you in contact with them this week!'[...] And that was incredible and just showed the kind of energy and enthusiasm our mentors had for us. [...] Any time I ever wanted to know more about anything, Carter would get back to me right away. He'd meet with us for lunch or after class to talk through things, and if he couldn't give us answers, he always knew who to ask in STEM AP and would connect us right away."

Our mentors care deeply about their mentees. It truly is as simple as that. Their caring translates into thoughtful reflections about how they can best help their mentees succeed in their STEM studies. For instance, Makayla's reflection illustrates the care peer mentors take in figuring out the best way to reach their mentees. "As a reflection for this week, I would love to share my mentoring experience with my mentees. I listened as my mentees shared thoughts and worries about 'goal confusion' and how they can achieve their goals while at college. I figured the most important thing that my mentees and other freshman and sophomore students could do to prepare for an effective and successful academic experience in college if they choose to pursue a science major, is to become clear about their goals and set up a solid goal during freshman or sophomore year at the latest. This solid goal needs to include what exact major you want to pursue (e.g. Biochemistry, Chemistry); why you want to pursue this major; what will be the plan after graduation (e.g. pursue PhD, med school, research work experience); what experience, skill sets, and knowledge you must have to prepare for your future plan; and how you are going to hone those skills or gain that knowledge. After figuring out this solid goal, it is much easier for science students to stay on track and achieve success by the time they graduate. This is what I shared with my mentees based on my own studying and working experience, and by sharing this, I hope to help my mentees figure out the answers to their worries about how to achieve their specific goals by the end of the undergraduate program at UMass."

With that sort of care and attention to a mentee's needs, how can our students not succeed!

One of the more common reflections on the value of peer mentors is exemplified in comments from Adam, an intense first-year student who pushed himself hard and often felt he came up short. "This week, I was super-stressed since I had a total of three exams and a quiz in organic chemistry. I knew what I had to do, yet I just could not bring myself to do so. However, during STEM AP, Danielle talked about her experiences in these same classes I am taking and it made me feel a lot better once she said that it gets easier. Though I am still struggling in organic chemistry, I feel a lot better in asking for help and going to the office when needed." Adam's mentor helped him understand that she had been in his shoes and survived. That sense of connection and the reassurance that things will get better had an immediate and positive impact on him. His level of anxiety dropped and his self-confidence increased. His reflection spoke to the impact beyond feeling a connection with his peer mentor; he now felt that he could ask for help in his organic chemistry course, something he had not felt comfortable doing before. This outcome is common among our first-year students as they spend time with their peer mentors. Their levels of self-confidence increase and they often begin to feel more comfortable asking for help; critically, asking for help outside of STEM AP. Their new confidence slowly begins to extend beyond their STEM AP comfort zone. This is precisely what our program seeks to accomplish!

Attention to the mentee's needs, willingness to help, and understanding of the mentee's goals are the core values instilled in all of our near-peer mentors. It is no surprise that many opportunities in life arise from knowing the right people and forming the right connections. But when you are a student in the minority, without a knowledgeable support network, it is often precisely those connections that are lacking. At the start of our bi-weekly near-peer mentor training sessions, each mentor is invited to share their life story. They are encouraged to provide detailed descriptions of their relevant experiences, professional opportunities, and campus involvement. Our training sessions not only strive to teach mentors how to build meaningful relationships with their mentees, but also help expose them to the richness of each other's experiences. We invite our mentors to acknowledge their accomplishments and, by sharing this information with other mentors, ensure that they bring this breadth and depth of experience to their mentoring relationships. Having this knowledge at their fingertips enables our mentors to feel more confident in their mentoring role, to become more effective mentors, and, as an added benefit, helps them realize how very much they have already experienced and accomplished.

"I definitely think the role of mentoring for me was really important, and after having done so many different things at UMass, I took it very seriously," mused Carter, a former STEM AP near-peer mentor. "I think it also made me more serious as a scientist and more accountable as a person. Even through STEM AP, I took this role of mentoring to mean more than just STEM AP. STEM AP kind of laid the groundwork for my attitude when it came to almost any space. Even when there were students that were my junior in the lab... I kind of took the opportunity to develop my mentoring skills in all areas. I found myself acting as a mentor even when I wasn't maybe being asked and just working to be a role model to a lot of students… just being someone that would speak up for the younger students when they maybe felt afraid or nervous to talk to a supervisor," he said.

Carter's passion for mentoring and advocacy for making every voice heard soon translated into his career endeavors. His research focused on water contaminants and when he discovered that his hometown's drinking water was contaminated with the same pollutants, he organized a community effort to address this health hazard. As an avid mentor and a gifted leader, he hoped to bring his knowledge and voice into international affairs and policy. "STEM AP and mentoring taught me that I have a greater responsibility to those around me, and that now, when I'm in a position of power or privilege or experience, or whatever it might be, I need to think about the people who aren't being spoken up for, the people who don't maybe understand everything that is going on and to make sure that anybody and everybody is being included when it comes to experience and knowledge. Because no matter what, we can't leave them behind." Since graduating, Carter is pursuing advanced studies in Environmental Engineering.

Our mentoring program does not focus solely on personal growth of the mentor and mentee, even though this is a critical goal. These students spend numerous hours focused on writing and refining their resumes, drafting personal statements, preparing for interviews, developing public speaking skills, and much more. We certainly see the connection with creating better, more finely tuned resumes and personal statements when students understand the significance and value inherent in their personal experiences that led to their personal growth. They are thereby better able to make the connection between those experiences and their own goals and aspirations. Our near-peer mentors take great pride in helping prepare their mentees to succeed in their college and professional ambitions. At the same time, these relationships provide opportunities for our mentors to reflect on and share the lessons and experiences they have acquired, and to practice their own leadership skills as they prepare to enter the workforce or pursue advanced studies. As they inspire their mentees, they are developing key personal skills, recognizing their own courage, and acknowledging the strength they have to face any adversity they encounter on their professional paths.

In order to see the mutual benefits of our near-peer mentor program, we need look no further than the final reflection from one of our beloved senior mentors Carter. "The true takeaway of peer mentoring is that it's really important to share with others what you learned, because your experiences aren't always unique to you. [...] It's like they say: It's not just about eating for yourself. It's about sharing your plate with others, especially when you are able to reap benefits of what you have sowed. I think giving back is huge because once you've figured something out, you can help the next person. You can be amazing and successful, but if you don't teach your friends and family how to eat, teach your people how to get to where you're at, or even better yet, how to surpass you, then you have to ask yourself: Did you really accomplish anything?"

Middle School Mentoring: Empowering the Mentor

Beyond providing mentors to STEM students, our program offers those same students the opportunity to engage in outreach activities with students in local middle schools. These activities provide our students with powerful experiences as they transition from student to teacher. They employ their knowledge, which they are often unaware they possess, to bring science alive for their mentees. In order to communicate the relevant science content, our mentors are trained to break down technical concepts and make them more accessible. There is no better way to learn than to teach, and our students quickly realize the challenge of translating their knowledge into meaningful experiences for these middle school students. Mentors engage their mentees in games, hands-on experiments, and skills development, all while highlighting their personal journeys, their understanding of the meaning of STEM, and their experiences in college, which the students love to hear.

"Middle school mentoring was actually one of the first things I heard about STEM AP that drew me to the program in the first place," noted Ethan, a senior STEM AP student. Ethan is a brilliant and caring student of biracial descent, who joined STEM AP as a second-year student in a nontraditional manner. His genuine nature and leadership qualities quickly led to his advancement to the role of program coordinator for STEM AP's middle school mentoring program. "When I think about my own life, it was the impact of older kids around me that really contributed to who I am today. And it really didn't take much at all. When you have someone to look up to, and you can see yourself in their shoes, well, that makes all the difference," he said. "Middle schoolers are also at this impressionable age where you can really start to build their love for science. You can shape the curiosity in them to really think about how the world works. [...] And from a mentor perspective, just learning how to work well with them and keep them engaged and involved, became incredibly rewarding for me."

Middle school children are perhaps the most challenging demographic to work with in our mentoring web. They are often high energy, with short attention spans and, for some, a keen need to have their voices heard. Our mentors must rapidly transform their approach to communicating science to meet these children's needs. As Ethan noted, "Through our program, we worked with students from the local public school district, pooling together students from four different elementary schools. And so, during our mentor trainings, we had to have a lot of open discussions on mentally and physically preparing new mentors before working with their mentees. Whenever there is a huge mix of students, you're going to be working with kids from all sorts of different backgrounds. For example, aside from their diversities in culture, race, and ethnicity, our program also had students at opposite ends of the socioeconomic scale. We had students coming from very high socioeconomic backgrounds and well-educated families, with parents who were both tenured professors at our university. But then, on the other side were students coming from very low socioeconomic status, single-parent households. [...] At times, these different backgrounds led to conflicts, and learning how to navigate and transform these situations into teaching moments was imperative," he remarked. Navigating these challenging mentoring experiences helps our students hone their communication skills and the ability to shift their approaches in real time, both of which are valuable skills for the workforce or future academic pursuits.

"When middle school mentoring was introduced to me during a seminar, I knew that was something I wanted to be a part of because I had experience working with kids and thought it was a great way to give back," reported Ruby. "Going through STEM AP helped increase my self-worth tremendously. [...] I used to be very insecure and lack confidence, but over time, STEM AP showed me that there are so many things that make me special and [that there are] many skills that I can bring to the table. I approached the then-leader of the Middle School Mentoring Program for a more active leadership role. [...] She right away noticed my initiative and desire to give back to the community and took me under her wing, allowing me to take on a leadership role in constructing the program itself. And so, I began working hand-in-hand with her and designing the experiments that the mentors and mentees would conduct, as well as the overall lesson plans and objectives for the experiments. [...] I feel like it has allowed me to gain a certain level of confidence in myself, in the way that I carry myself, in the way I present myself, and in the way that I speak to others."

Our middle school mentors extensively prepare materials for use in engaging their mentees in science activities. This often gives them a pause, demanding reflection and critical thinking, especially if they're dealing with an unfamiliar topic outside their field. Students often report feeling anxious and uncertain at the outset. They doubt at first whether they will be successful at engaging middle school students, but then quickly learn that once the mentoring sessions begin, their sense of self-efficacy increases, as does their enjoyment of the mentoring activity.

"The Middle School Mentoring Program is actually what first drew me to joining STEM AP," asserted Taylor, a recent graduate from our program at UMass.

As a first-generation college student and Pell Grant recipient, Taylor had joined STEM AP in search of community and the chance to help guide younger students as they navigate their way through some of the challenges she had experienced. "Growing up, I was part of Girls Inc., which is a mentoring program for all girls, and I started going there when I was 7," she said. "I just loved working with the younger girls and being a mentor to them. So when I heard about STEM AP, I was like, 'Oh this is great! It'll make Amherst a home away from home!' I've now been in the program for four years. It has honestly been such a blessing for me in every way possible. [...] The Middle School Mentoring Program was interesting because we were challenged to think about ways to make each topic more interesting: like how do you really engage these young students on a physics lesson about Newton's Laws? Sometimes, the students would get easily irritated or it was hard to get their attention, but once we started talking to them and started the hands-on demonstrations, they suddenly became so calm and interested! They would ask you questions, and you would really see their excitement and that was my most favorite thing. [...] I really loved working with the kids because they're just so innocent and pure. [...] And, as a mentor, when you meet the kids, they look up to you and they think you can do anything. And I think that's amazing, because when you have those self-doubts, and you hear the kids be like, 'Oh, you're so smart, I want to be like you,' it's just so motivating and inspiring... it just makes me want to work harder at what I'm doing. [...] And so just seeing how much my STEM AP mentors and mentees believed in me became so important to helping me believe in myself." Taylor recently graduated but has remained at UMass to pursue an advanced degree in Genetics. She has also remained active in STEM AP, acting as a graduate student mentor and serving on the leadership team.

Taylor's dedication to her students and her insightful self-reflections highlight the valuable skills the Middle School Mentoring Program imparts to our student mentors. The impact of these mentoring experiences is shared by many of our middle school mentors. "Being a part of middle school mentoring felt really great because I was not only helping students engage more with science, but I was also helping students in my very own community. [...] It was really about helping these young people be interested and engaged in science and that felt really great to do. [...] Throughout the program, we did all types of activities with them, each with different science lessons. [...] We would play games with them right before the program started, like, if we got there early, we'd do all these different really fun activities that let me channel the kid within me while building a stronger relationship with the students," exclaimed Carter.

"As a first-generation college student, the thought of college was exciting but also scary at the same time," reflected Sofia, an upper-year student majoring in Biochemistry and Molecular Biology. "I was going to be the first female Latina from my family to go to a four-year university and study medicine. I knew I was in over my head, but I continued to pursue my dreams, which is to study medicine. Coming to UMass was a huge jump for me. And by being at such a huge college like UMass Amherst... well, one can get lost in all the noise. But I managed to find a community in STEM AP. [...] Through STEM AP, I mentored middle school students weekly, and while mentoring them, we did scientific experiments to explore different science areas. [...] This type of outreach was very important to me, because I have gained so much knowledge and got to be so involved in my community because of it. [...] It's what showed what else was out there for me in the world."

We frequently hear our STEM Ambassadors speak about the importance of mentoring in helping them believe in themselves. These experiences are often transformative. "Ever since I was young, I always wanted to be a doctor and help people in that manner, especially after being a witness to their importance. I lived in Beirut, Lebanon, for most of my life and witnessed crises firsthand, ranging from ambulance workers rushing to the scene of an explosion, to an orthopedic surgeon restoring my mom's ability to walk after a car accident. Doctors have always held a place in my heart, and I want to be able to help others in the same manner that they helped those closest to me," said Raphael, an upper-year student of Arabic and Hispanic descent majoring in Biochemistry and Molecular Biology. "Students who were once in our shoes acted as our peer mentors and introduced us to the importance of reflecting on ourselves and sharing with others. [...] Then middle school mentoring happened... I was asked to take what I learned in my STEM major and use that to mentor middle school students. We would carry out activities with them, ranging from lab tours to figuring out how to solve problems collectively. This was difficult with middle schoolers, but the fact that we were able to positively influence their perspective on science and encourage them to pursue STEM fields in the future was important to me. [...] Looking back, STEM AP has given me crucial experiences, guidance, and a community, things which I never expected to obtain when I enrolled in the 'small' one-credit course."

The Transformative Power of Mentoring

We cannot overstate the role mentoring plays in helping our students develop and succeed in their STEM studies. In STEM AP, we purposely created an interconnected mentoring network that derives much of its power from our AMR mentoring model. We focus on developing affinity, mutuality, and reciprocity in all of our mentoring relationships. This unique perspective, in which we celebrate how both the mentor and mentee bring valuable knowledge, resources, and life experiences to the relationship, can make all the difference in our students' growth as STEM professionals. From their very first meeting, our younger students are invited to share their stories and view themselves as a resource, with much to offer their fellow mentees and even their mentors! STEM AP students are routinely and repeatedly invited to help and be helped by each other. As they transition into mentoring roles themselves, their confidence and professionalism grow rapidly. They are encouraged to view their life experiences and their cultural norms as providing richness and knowledge, rather than as something from which they should distance themselves or leave behind in the dorm room or at home. It is with this philosophy and these values that our mentor and mentee relationships become so powerful and mutually beneficial.

References

1. Eldeleklioglu, J. The Relationship Between the Perceived Social Support and the Level of Depression and Anxiety in University Students. *Kuram Ve Uygulamada Egitim Bilim.* **2006**, *6* (3), 742–752.
2. American College Health Association, *National College Health Assessment II: Reference Group Executive Summary Fall*; American College Health Association: Hanover, MD, 2017.
3. Stephens, N. M.; Townsend, S. S. M.; Markus, H. R.; Phillips, L. T. A Cultural Mismatch: Independent Cultural Norms Produce Greater Increases in Cortisol and More Negative Emotions among First-Generation College Students. *J. Exp. Soc. Psychol.* **2012**, *48* (6), 1389–1393. DOI:10.1016/j.jesp.2012.07.008.
4. Ellis, J. M.; Powell, C. S.; Demetriou, C. P.; Huerta-Bapat, C.; Panter, A. T. Examining First-Generation College Student Lived Experiences With Microaggressions and Microaffirmations at a Predominately White Public Research University. *Cultur. Divers. Ethn. Minor. Psychol.* **2019**, *25* (2), 266–279. DOI:10.1037/cdp0000198.
5. *The Steve Fund and JED Launch Equity in Mental Health Framework to Support College Students of Color;* JED Foundation. https://www.jedfoundation.org/steve-fund-jed-launch-equity-mental-health-framework-support-college-students-color/ access date: January 15, 2021.
6. Head, L.; Lindsey, J. Anxiety and the University Student: A Brief Review of the Professional Literature. *Coll. Stud. J.* **1983**, *17* (2), 176–182.
7. Sithole, A.; Chiyaka, E. T.; McCarthy, P.; Mupinga, D. M.; Bucklein, B. K.; Kibirige, J. Student Attraction, Persistence and Retention in STEM Programs: Successes and Continuing Challenges. *High. Educ. Stud.* **2017**, *7* (1), 46. DOI:10.5539/hes.v7n1p46.
8. Rice, K. G.; Ray, M. E.; Davis, D. E.; DeBlaere, C.; Ashby, J. S. Perfectionism and Longitudinal Patterns of Stress for STEM Majors: Implications for Academic Performance. *J. Couns. Psychol.* **2015**, *62* (4), 718–731. DOI:10.1037/cou0000097.
9. Henry, M. A.; Shorter, S.; Charkoudian, L.; Heemstra, J. M.; Corwin, L. A. *FAIL* Is Not a Four-Letter Word: A Theoretical Framework for Exploring Undergraduate Students' Approaches to Academic Challenge and Responses to Failure in STEM Learning Environments. *CBE Life Sci. Educ.* **2019**, *18* (1), Ar.11. DOI:10.1187/cbe.18-06-0108.
10. Bryerly, A. A Quantitative Study of the Source of Stress for First Generation Freshman Female. Masters Thesis. Eastern Illinois University, Charleston, Ill, U.S.A, **2016**.
11. Leary, M.; Morewood, A.; Bryner, R. A Controlled Intervention to Improve Freshman Retention in a STEM-Based Physiology Major. *Adv. Physiol. Educ.* **2020**, *44* (3), 334–343. DOI:10.1152/advan.00038.2020.
12. Committee on Barriers and Opportunities in Completing 2-Year and 4-Year STEM Degrees; Board on Science Education; Policy and Global Affairs; National Academy of Engineering; National Academies of Sciences, Engineering, and Medicine. In: Malcom, S., Feder, M., Eds. Barriers and Opportunities for 2-Year and 4-Year STEM Degrees: Systemic Change to Support Students' Diverse Pathways; National Academies Press: Washington, DC, 2016, p 21739. DOI:10.17226/21739.

13. Curchoe, C. L. The Power of Mentoring. *Science* **2015**, *350* (6259), 478–478. DOI:10.1126/science.350.6259.478.
14. Tenenbaum, L. S.; Anderson, M. K.; Jett, M.; Yourick, D. L. An Innovative Near-Peer Mentoring Model for Undergraduate and Secondary Students: STEM Focus. *Innov. High Educ.* **2014**, *39* (5), 375–385. DOI:10.1007/s10755-014-9286-3.
15. Cook, L.; Mentor/*Mentee Relationships: The Experience of African American STEM Majors* Order No. 3626242 Morgan State University, 2014. Ann Arbor: ProQuest [Web]. 8 Jan. 2021; Morgan State University: Ann Arbor, MI, 2021.
16. Estrada, M.; Hernandez, P. R.; Schultz, P. W. A Longitudinal Study of How Quality Mentorship and Research Experience Integrate Underrepresented Minorities Into STEM Careers. *CBE Life Sci. Educ.* **2018**, *17* (1), Ar.9. DOI:10.1187/cbe.17-04-0066.
17. Stelter, R. L.; Kupersmidt, J. B.; Stump, K. N. Establishing Effective STEM Mentoring Relationships Through Mentor Training. *Ann. N.Y. Acad. Sci.* **2021**, *1483* (1), 224–243. DOI:10.1111/nyas.14470.
18. Pfund, C. *Entering Mentoring*, 1st ed.; W. H. Freeman and Company: New York, NY, 2014.

Chapter 4

Research Experience: A Nearly Perfect Predictor of STEM Student Success

Engaging in Research

Engaging in research is one of the best predictors of STEM degree completion.[1–3] STEM students need—and want—to engage in research to develop their own STEM identity, immerse themselves in the culture of STEM, and explore the many opportunities this training provides.[4] More specifically, they want to "join a lab," which is a common refrain coming from students entering our program. However, there are two challenges that limit our ability to provide authentic, engaging research experiences. First, there simply aren't enough research opportunities to accommodate all undergraduate STEM students who want them. Equally important, and yet rarely discussed, is the fact that research faculty must actively create and foster a laboratory culture that provides an inclusive, engaging experience if they intend to train the diversity of STEM students who wish for such experiences.[3]

Santiago joined our program as an enthusiastic first-year student. He had intentions of being a successful science student, but was unsure of exactly what to do, apart from striving to get good grades. His reasons for joining STEM Ambassadors Program (STEM AP) certainly included wanting to join a research lab, but in his case, an equally important part of the decision was his desire to be part of a diverse community focused on STEM. Santiago was fortunate to earn a STEM AP summer Research Experiences for Undergraduates (REU) and his reflections reveal the power of that experience. "I think it goes without saying that times like these can get extremely frustrating: when nothing works out despite all your planning and feeling as if you have no control over your projects. Yes, it's annoying, but I feel this is something everyone has to go through eventually." Santiago went on to talk about his experience as a budding lab researcher, saying, "I can't imagine a world where someone's experiment always goes exactly as they wanted, exactly as expected, without ever facing complications. These are things I have to learn to accept: sometimes things won't work out the way I want them to, but I need to acknowledge where

Empowering Underrepresented Students in Science. DOI: http://dx.doi.org/10.1016/B978-0-323-90469-8.00004-4

I went wrong, and build myself up from there." Santiago worked through his frustrations, persevered, and ultimately reached his research goals. This experience of trying and failing and trying again was fundamentally important to his growth as a scientist.

And Santiago is not the exception. Time and again, we hear students who are "lucky" enough to gain a research experience describe that experience as transformative.[5] Clearly, we must provide this key ingredient for all our STEM students, but there is a catch.

It's a Numbers Game

Unfortunately, for most students, especially those of the demographic our program serves, gaining an undergraduate research opportunity is highly unlikely. Even factoring in the increasing availability of summer REUs,[6] the majority of STEM students miss out on this opportunity. Further, the relatively few research posts available generally go to the students who are the most informed and prepared to go after them. For the underserved majority, opportunities pass by because they have no idea how to pursue a research position or are unaware how important it is for them to acquire such experiences. However, this is starting to change, in part through the leadership of the National Science Foundation (NSF), which has advocated for and funded an increasing number of REU opportunities, which preferentially accept applications from URMs[7].

How bad is this situation? Let's use our own institution, the University of Massachusetts Amherst, as an example. The Department of Biology has 43 faculty, of which 30 are active in research, and about 1500 students who declare Biology as their major. If we were to offer a research opportunity to every student who wanted one, each faculty member would need to admit 25 or so students each year into their laboratories. In contrast, the typical faculty member hosts just one to three undergraduate students per year. There simply aren't enough research opportunities to accommodate the vast majority of students who want one.

In the early days of our program, we ensured each student was admitted to a research lab. Students flocked to our program, in part because they heard we could help them join a lab. As our program grew more rapidly than we had anticipated, however, this guarantee became untenable. In fact, one of our program's first growing pains was that we had so many students we couldn't keep up with the demand for research opportunities. We needed another approach and we found one in CUREs.

What Are CUREs, Anyway?

Course-Based Undergraduate Research Experiences (CUREs) are class-based authentic research experiences that serve as a highly effective proxy for a traditional lab-based research position.[8] A well-configured CURE, such as those our program offers, provides opportunities for students to collaborate with each other, ask questions and challenge each other and their instructor, and make discoveries on their own while learning the hands-on, practical, and applicable nature of the science.[9] By design, students tackle real-world problems that matter to them, generate novel data, and communicate their findings to others.[10] CUREs bring science alive for students.

Abby enrolled in one of our CUREs during her first semester of college. She quickly learned that there was something special about the experience. "The CURE research allowed me and my peers to tackle a very real-world epidemic of antibiotic resistance in mutated bacteria. I love tackling challenges that are happening in the world today and researching new methods to potentially save the world with new scientific discoveries." Her classmate, Eva, felt similarly: "These activities made me feel like I am an individual working to help the greater good through elite research and being a part of a team with a greater goal: to learn and to help society."

What was particularly special was that in contrast to most of their arm's-length STEM classes, the CURE engaged them in a topic about which they quickly became passionate, offered them the opportunity to design a novel experiment, generate new data, and make sense of what they found. STEM classes, particularly in the first few years of college, are often large and highly competitive, and frequently cover topics that may seem irrelevant to students' experiences. Further, most are still taught in the traditional style of a professor expounding at the front of a large lecture hall as students quietly absorb the material. Laboratory experiences associated with these large lecture courses usually involve prescriptive or "cookbook" activities that do not expose students to scientific discovery.[11] These lab courses are certainly more intimate than the lecture halls, with 20 to 30 students gathering in a laboratory setting. However, students are given a "recipe" and required to follow those instructions, and their resulting data is compared with what the instructor, usually a graduate teaching assistant (TA), knows the correct answer to be. The exercise is not authentic research and is usually not chosen to align with the student's interests. Further, the TAs generally do not receive training on how to engage students or provide an inclusive laboratory experience.[12] Numerous studies have shown that far more students fail STEM courses when the materials are offered solely in this fashion.[13,14] If this is the only exposure to a research experience most STEM students get, it is no wonder that so many seek other fields to engage their passion and intellect.

In contrast, a CURE is designed to be engaging and highly relevant to the student, and to bring science alive. CUREs invite students to produce novel data related to topics that are relevant to their interests. In contrast to traditional laboratory courses, CUREs are not simply offered to provide experience with a particular skill set. Equally important, students often get to know, and learn directly from, the research scientists themselves. This is a live instance of a scientist bringing their passion for science directly to the student. How cool is that?

Ruby enrolled in our CURE in her first semester of college and instantly felt the power of engaging in real-world science with a team of peers. As she put it: "... to be put in smaller groups where I had to meet with people and work together on something [...] it made me feel right out of the gate that I was a person and not just a number, which was honestly really amazing. Also, just learning more about current topics, specifically antibiotic resistance, was incredible."

Creating a CURE

It was daunting to realize we needed an entirely new approach if we hoped to provide enough research opportunities for the growing number of students in our program. We had filled all the available research labs, and yet, more students kept coming. As Aesop's fable cautions, "Be careful what you wish for."[15] We had wished for a large, diverse, highly engaged community of scholars, and now here it was; and it demanded more resources than we had available. We scrambled to provide an alternative research experience for half of our first-year students by inviting them to participate in our very first CURE.

Despite the urgency, creating the CURE was much less stressful than we had anticipated, as we will reveal below. To begin, we picked a topic we had experience with and that we knew would resonate with our students: the global challenge of antibiotic resistance. However, if you feel intimidated by the thought of creating a brand-new, authentic research experience for your own students, there are numerous CURES available as open-source teaching materials for faculty to adapt to their needs. The CUREnet website is one resource devoted to providing curated CURES that faculty can download for their own use.[16] Each CURE includes a course syllabus, an introduction to the topic, detailed instructions for required materials, a proposed grading rubric for assessment, and advice for implementation. The range of available CURE topics is rapidly expanding,[17,18] as is the data indicating that CUREs offer a powerful tool for improving science knowledge and achievement, particularly for students typically underrepresented in STEM fields.[18,19]

Based upon our students' needs, we chose to create a CURE that required two hours in the laboratory each week, followed by one hour of assignments. This ensured students could fit the CURE into their already full schedules. We then drafted a curriculum that focused on meeting the following objectives: (i) introduce students to basic laboratory skills; (ii) teach them to read research articles; (iii) provide them with an authentic research experience; (iv) develop their communication skills by requiring them to present their results in the form of a poster; and (v) help them understand the power of working in teams. It sounds like a full curriculum, and it is, but what was surprising was how all of this content comfortably fit into our three-hour-per-week format over the course of 13 weeks.

Day 1 of our CURE starts with a brief introduction to the challenge of antibiotic resistance and invites the students to begin exploring the relevant scientific literature. The rest of the first session is spent learning how to use standard laboratory equipment, such as Bunsen burners, pipettes, and scales. By the second meeting, students are required to take charge of the conversation and are invited to share their own experiences using antibiotics.

The first time we offered this CURE, and every time since, we witnessed an extraordinary outcome on this second day. It was like opening a floodgate. After a brief, awkward moment of silence, the students started to talk. They shared their experiences with infectious diseases and their anxieties about increasing levels of antibiotic resistance. They even shared how they felt knowing that these precious medicines are used by the agricultural industry to increase food production levels. They wanted to keep sharing and we encouraged them to do so. Of course, there are always a few students who are reticent to join in. We addressed this challenge directly by requesting that the entire group take responsibility for ensuring that every student became a part of the conversation. Students immediately turned to each other, encouraging each other to contribute. By the end of this first student-led conversation, they were hooked!

Over the following weeks, our students practiced laboratory techniques while reading relevant research articles, learned how to keep a lab notebook, and began to design an experiment replete with all the necessary controls. During this transition period, the instructor plays a far more passive role than is often typical, watching and commenting as students navigate their way through the exercises. As a result of this hands-off approach to oversight, the students make mistakes; many, many mistakes. Their experiments fail. They forget to incorporate proper controls. They forget to assign a team member to check on the progress of their experiment outside of class. Every conceivable failure occurs, as well as many that we had not conceived! But this is part of the process. The key to a successful CURE is to require students to figure out how to learn from their mistakes and move forward. This critical experience of self-reliance is what makes a CURE magical, as Joyce describes below.

Joyce is a transfer student from a local community college. Although she did well at her original college, she was still very uncertain about how she would manage to find a community and be able to thrive in the daunting environment of a research institution. As she put it, "One thing that was challenging—like, really challenging—was analyzing our mistakes and coming up with the explanations for why our data came out the way it did. But since it was all up to us, we really had to think hard to come up with a good explanation for why our data showed what it did and our goals through teamwork…"

By the third week, students were placed in small groups and invited to come up with a research project related to antibiotic resistance. Each time the CURE is offered, the specific focus of the research changes, but when Joyce participated, the course's main focus was antibiotic resistance in food contaminants. Each team had to decide what food to sample and how to sample it. Joyce was placed in a team that included a particularly diverse cross-section of students. She had never experienced a team-based approach to learning before and was fearful; she felt merely communicating might be hard, particularly because two of her teammates were non-native English speakers. They did struggle at first, but a powerful and passionate team emerged rather quickly. Soon, Joyce realized how potent this approach could be. "What was nice is we would commit to meet together outside of class and we would always show up and never compromise anyone's thoughts. [...] Whatever thoughts anyone shared were always good and then, if someone had a better idea, we would all agree to say, 'Okay, let's talk about both of them and analyze them together.' I really hadn't done that before. And this was really awesome because it made me like research even more."

Amira, who is now a STEM AP graduate and a former student leader, initially joined the CURE to gain experience that would make her more competitive in securing a research laboratory position. She recalled, "I participated in a CURE my first year because coming out of high school, I didn't feel confident in my laboratory skills. I didn't know how to pipette or any of those basic skills that I knew I would want to learn, especially if I want to be a competitive applicant in a summer research program or to be a member of a lab. So that was one of my main reasons for joining."

One of her biggest surprises was the challenge of working in a team. The look on her face when she realized she had to work with other students was priceless. Amira is headstrong and has always relied on herself to succeed. Now, though, she had to find a way to work with other students who had completely different styles and talents. It took a while for her to adapt and her reflections make things sound considerably easier than they actually were for her! "One of the biggest things that I realized was that we have to work together. That was new for me. It was a little bit of a challenge but I got the hang of it because coming into first year, I didn't know anybody, so I felt weird starting research with people I didn't even know. But it ended up turning out fine toward the end."

The CURE runs for one semester and consists of 13 two-hour class periods. About half of those sessions occur in an introductory biology lab room where the students sample bacteria and assess levels of antibiotic resistance. They quickly take ownership of their projects and are completely responsible for producing results. The final phase involves producing a poster describing their study and then presenting it to their peers. One of the more memorable moments for us was watching our first class of CURE students present their posters at a local STEM conference. It just so happened that a former NSF director was in attendance; she spent several hours with our students, examining their posters. She made it a point to speak with us after, noting, "I truly thought these were graduate students, until you reminded me they were first semester freshmen. It is amazing that they have come so far in just two months in your CURE."

For those who teach first-year college students, this story may sound implausible. How can you take 20 first-semester college students, turn them loose on a science project they know almost nothing about, and have a productive, intense learning experience in such a short time? Impossible, right? And yet, each time we offer this CURE, we have the same experience: our students are instantly engaged, they learn, they explore, they work in teams, and they emerge in a different state, more confident in their abilities. In short, they feel like scientists.

One of our first critical findings was that the key to a successful CURE is not the amount of research performed, but, rather, that the research is new, authentic, and owned by the students.[11,20,21] A CURE doesn't just offer opportunities to investigate interesting phenomena; it is also part of a process that builds upon a student's practical exposure to scientific inquiry. It teaches research protocols, provides opportunities for collaboration and problem solving, and develops students' leadership and communication skills, among several other very pertinent skills. Students report that they love the teamwork and the relationship they build with their peers, noting that it helps them rely on each other and trust what each is doing despite wanting to do things their own way.

As described by Caroline, "The CURE is still one of the most interesting and engaging classes I have ever enrolled in. I remember around four weeks into the course, I felt I had learned more from that one class than any of my other classes combined. In this course, I gained so many technical skills that helped me feel comfortable and confident in future lab courses. I also gained more soft skills and self-awareness that now enable me to work better in groups and be a more thorough student."

Osa reflected even earlier in the semester on her CURE experience and how it provided a supportive, inclusive experience that welcomed diverse perspectives and approaches. "This week, we had to collaborate as a class to come up with a research topic. Everyone had different approaches to the kind of research they came up with. This activity taught me that even though someone has a perspective different from yours, that doesn't mean you cannot work together. It simply means that they are bringing something different to the table and different ideas can create something big and amazing. In science, teamwork is very important, and I am learning every day to be more open-minded and supportive."

Leah, a shy first-year student, was overwhelmed by the CURE format at first. However, by the end of the course, he was a vocal contributor to our group reflection. In particular, he was convinced that teamwork was the most important aspect of the CURE. This was his first experience working in a team and he noted in one reflection that it felt great to work in a team because you didn't need to know it all. In his words, "If you weren't strong in math, someone else might be. If you don't know how to use Excel, there would be someone on the team who was an Excel wizard!"

For Jessie, an energetic first-year student, the CURE experience made a STEM career seem more appealing and approachable: "These activities are sparking my interest in the STEM field even more than before. The more involved I am becoming, the more I am fascinated and engaged, which is causing my desire to have a career in the STEM field to grow even more."

As stressed earlier, the CURE experience is quite different from a traditional lab course. It is authentic; in other words, the problem tackled is real and the students engage in a research process that is identical to that which occurs in research laboratories. In most lab courses, the instructors already know the answer and have created a recipe for the students to follow. In a CURE, the data generated are novel and no one knows what will be found before the course begins. Hence, its appeal!

Mary, a second-year Microbiology major, reflected on the importance of having to think independently in her CURE. "In my CURE... we practiced more with planning and conducting our own experiments. This part of the class is both helpful and challenging. In the short term, it's hard not having as much guidance, but I know in the long term it will help us all [become] better researchers who can be more efficient and think on [our] feet."

Caroline also felt that the CURE made her think in novel ways. "We were given very minimal instructions and had to create our own question, hypothesis, and procedure. As a result, I collaborated with my partners to decide what exactly we wanted to test for, and how we would go about doing this. I was able to see my abilities with regard to the various STEM skills we had discussed the week prior, and I was able to see first-hand in context which skills I truly did have, which ones still needed more work, and which skills were completely lost to me." Caroline was taking a traditional chemistry lab at the same time as her CURE, and she also reflected on the difference between the two. "In Chemistry, we are given the procedures, the TA knows the results we should end up with, and we are all doing practically the same thing, so we are able to use other people's data when our own does not work. In CURE, we create our experiments and have to be creative with our thinking. We can hypothesize what our results should be, but there is no set answer, unlike my chemistry lab."

In addition to engaging them in the process of science, CUREs provide opportunities for students to integrate into the STEM culture and gain a sense of ownership of their project, which has been shown to motivate students, even when faced with challenges.[22] The students begin to think and act like STEM professionals, and that is when the real magic occurs!

Let's return to Santiago, who attended a CURE and then leveraged that experience to join a research lab. Here was a student who had expressed fear and uncertainty about working in a lab. Yet, he took the CURE and was transformed. His use of scientific language, his demeanor, command of scientific processes, and ability to clearly communicate those processes without fear and hesitation, speak volumes of the sense of self-efficacy he gained from participation in a CURE. What participation in CUREs did for Osa, Santiago, and so many other students, it could do for thousands of students who never get the chance to experience research as a college student. We know what happens when they fail to get these experiences: more than half of STEM students switch majors or drop out of college. Meanwhile, those in the CURE learn both the hard science *and* the soft skills of teamwork and collaboration, communication, and problem-solving. Moreover, they learn that science can be unpredictable—even frustrating—but that is all part of the process. They learn to hang loose; they learn to be *human* while doing science!

CUREs as a Solution

It is hard to believe that a student who participates in a very short-term CURE might gain more than one who is ensconced in a research lab, but this is often the case. The reason, in retrospect, is obvious: the CURE is intentionally designed to be an inclusive educational research experience that, when done well, ensures each student's voice is heard and their individual needs met. Equally importantly, students gain training and experience in the most critical technical aspects of research. In contrast, when an undergraduate student enters a research lab, they are often relegated to washing dishes or making solutions, all valuable skills to learn, no doubt, but not authentic research. In many labs, students are sometimes treated as a nuisance until they have learned enough to actually generate data. If they survive the servitude stage, they may then work for a graduate student or post-doc who was never trained in mentoring, who may not want to work with the student, and who has their own needs (which generally come first). What students learn, how they learn it, and how they experience this learning will vary widely from lab to lab and from mentor to mentor.

Here, we address the second challenge posed at the start of this chapter. To be successful in engaging and retaining students, particularly URM students, the instructor or principal investigator (PI) must actively create and lead a laboratory culture that provides an inclusive, engaging experience. In this sense, STEM AP produced magic for more than just the students! Before we created STEM AP and developed our first CUREs, Prof. Riley, who is active in research and runs a fairly large lab, is embarrassed to reveal that she ran her lab very much like your typical research-driven enterprise. In the traditional model, the "PI" runs the show, but is often removed from the day-to-day research activities and may never interact with the undergraduates helping out. PIs focus on grant writing, publishing, and training graduate students and post-docs. Mentoring and training undergraduates, unfortunately, often falls far down on their to-do list.

Prof. Riley can say, sadly, that for the first 15 years of her tenure at Yale University, it was rare for her to know the names of the undergraduates working in her lab, much less provide them with instruction or mentoring. Considering that she was juggling numerous research projects, multiple grants, and her own research, as well as overseeing the research of three to four graduate students and a post-doc or two, it is perhaps easier to understand this failure on her part. However, she was also never incentivized to train undergraduates. In fact, doing so was often considered a drain on her resources and time. Students were assigned to a graduate student or post-doc… and, well, honestly, she felt her job was done. She never worried about precisely what those students did in the lab, as she was certain it would be a great experience for the students to simply be there. How differently she feels now, having helped create STEM AP and developed her first CURE. In her CUREs, she focuses on ensuring each student is heard and acknowledged, in addition to making sure each student gains mastery of the basic skills and participates in class conversations.

In contrast to many research experiences, CUREs not only make research accessible to far more students, they also ensure that those students all receive training in a core set of skills to ensure they develop their research proficiency and STEM identity, and that they all share equally in the instructor's focus and mentorship. Even more importantly, their contributions are valued from the first day of the CURE; they are the focus of the research experience, not an afterthought.

The impact of this approach is almost unimaginable. Asia found that the CURE affected her in numerous ways, from science knowledge to STEM identity. "I participated in a CURE class that was like an introduction to research and how to think like a scientist. I learned so much about myself. I gained confidence to speak out and lead a group. I also gained knowledge about a subject I did not know a lot about, and most importantly, I learned that I can be a scientist. Science is what I love and where I want to be."

Why Haven't CUREs Taken Off?

CUREs are a relatively new approach to engaging students in research, and it is taking time to convince faculty that they are as powerful an educational tool as we have experienced in our program. Many instructors feel CUREs are too much work to create, or that their research is not amenable to a CURE format, or perhaps they don't like the idea of not being in control of the classroom.[23] Some are simply overwhelmed with their current responsibilities: running their research labs, teaching students, and engaging in university service.[24] However, what they may be missing in their consideration of adopting CUREs is the fact that these courses provide an invaluable opportunity for scientists to meet and identify the most promising young researchers and, perhaps, invite them to join their lab.

Research faculty crave highly motivated and proficient undergraduates to help in their research enterprises. How to find the best of these students, however, presents a challenge. It is often a matter of serendipity. Perhaps a student took your course, or sent an unsolicited email, or just bumped into you in the hall. In each case, you are taking a chance on that student, and someone in your lab will invest a significant amount of energy to train the student, with a reasonable probability that this particular student won't fit into your lab environment or may not find your research that interesting after all. Imagine that instead of a random walk among student trainees, you were able to observe them for several months and identify those most perfectly suited to your research focus and style. No more guessing if a student will fit the bill based on a single conversation or on how they did on an exam, or even that they were brave enough to approach you. Instead, you watch them work in a team and demonstrate proficiency in basic laboratory skills, then listen to them explain their research back to you. Even if this were the only reason for offering a CURE, it would be a pretty compelling one.

Some faculty doubt their ability to translate their research into a CURE, or perhaps they are not active in research and thus feel they couldn't offer a CURE.

We encountered precisely this situation in STEM AP. The program director is a STEM educator, not a research scientist, and yet, she wanted to engage our students in a CURE focused on the STEM workforce development needs of the Caribbean islands, where she had grown up. We brainstormed for several weeks on how to make this happen. Never one to let hurdles impede her, she connected with a scientist focused on water quality in Haiti and convinced him to help her create a CURE that combined their interests. The result was a CURE that brought Haitian history, culture, and political unrest to bear on the critical need to develop a STEM workforce, while simultaneously providing training in laboratory techniques required to tackle the health challenge of ensuring a safe water source free from contamination from cholera-causing bacteria. The plan was for this CURE to culminate with an REU opportunity for several students to spend the summer in Haiti engaged in cholera research and communicating with local community members about the importance of safe water practices. Political unrest caused us to abort the REU, but the CURE itself was a smashing success. Again, this wasn't because of the amount of research; it was because the students, several of whom were of Haitian heritage themselves, were passionate about that research. They had experienced the need for safe water in their own upbringing and were committed to helping Haitians address this challenge.

There is yet another path to providing CUREs that does not require faculty to invest their time in creating and testing a new lab course. As mentioned previously, CUREnet is a nonprofit organization that enables networking among faculty who are developing, teaching, and assessing CUREs; shares CURE projects and resources; and develops new tools and strategies for CURE instruction and assessment.[16] Our Biology Department has chosen to use one of these existing CUREs—SEA-PHAGES,[25] which engages students in hunting for viruses—to provide an authentic research experience for the 1400 students who enroll in an introductory biology course each fall. Instructing this vast number of students requires that graduate TAs, rather than PIs, oversee the students' research efforts. The leaders of this program recognize the importance of ensuring the TAs receive extensive training, not only in the science behind the CURE, but in how to create an engaging, inclusive laboratory environment. This effort is brand-new and the jury is still out with respect to how inspiring this "en masse" approach will be. However, if this venture proves successful, think about all the students who stand to gain a critical research experience during their first year! From our perspective, the ability to engage such large numbers of students in authentic research in their first year at college is what makes CUREs one of the most attractive solutions to date, to the challenge of providing research opportunities for all STEM students.

One doesn't have to adopt CUREs in the aggressive manner that our department has, to have a significant impact on the student body. Imagine a department in which each faculty member offered one CURE each year. In our department alone, this would mean that 600 students would have the opportunity to engage in real research. In this vision, STEM faculty would instantly provide what we know to be the greatest predictor of success in STEM studies: an authentic research experience. What an amazing step forward this would be!

Getting Into a Research Laboratory

A major goal for most of our students is joining a research lab. We mentioned above several challenges associated with gaining access to these coveted positions: the limited number of lab slots available, the networking required to find an opening, and the self-confidence one must possess to put oneself out there and compete with one's peers for this limited resource. Students of the demographics our program serves are particularly affected by these challenges. Many do not realize, until late in their undergraduate careers, the importance of gaining research experience and the transformative nature of research on their growth as scientists. Others, having mustered the courage to submit an application, get discouraged after a single rejection, and may not realize that it often takes numerous attempts to finally connect with the right lab at the right time.

STEM AP directly addresses this challenge through our graduate mentoring program. We encourage our mentors to help their mentees navigate what is to most an invisible network of research opportunities. To begin, they introduce their students to the scientific literature and teach them how to work through dense, often overwhelming, research articles. Mentors also help their mentees understand the concept of experimental design, the need for experimental replication, and the necessity of maintaining a detailed laboratory notebook. In short, they expose them to some of the basic skills involved in engaging in real research. Most of our mentors also physically place their students in their own research spaces, demystifying the aura surrounding research labs. Students begin to realize that behind those locked doors are people just like them: engaged in the self-driven pursuit of knowledge.

Mentors also teach their students the mechanics of gaining access to a research lab. They have their mentees practice composing introductory emails to potential PIs and help them navigate setbacks. Mentors make clear that few students are instantly granted access to a lab position. They share their stories of being rejected from a lab or choosing to leave labs they weren't comfortable in. In many cases, the graduate mentors may see potential in a particular student, inviting them to join their lab and work directly with them. We had naturally hoped for that outcome in a few cases, but never dreamed it would end up being as common an occurrence as it has proven to be.

As we describe above, different laboratories provide students with a broad range of learning environments. It remains true that most STEM research faculty received their training in a fairly traditional way: as an apprentice within a rigidly hierarchical laboratory organization and power structure. When they have the opportunity to create their own laboratory environments, they often emulate those they experienced as graduate students and post-docs. These new faculty are not trained in how to recognize an inclusive and engaging lab environment, much less produce one of their own. In contrast, they often adhere to the dominant mantra: that a successful researcher is independent, competitive, and driven to succeed against all odds. In this schema, undergraduates must learn how to navigate what remains a predominately individualistic, hierarchical, and extremely competitive research space. Additionally, students must learn that different labs have varying rules, both explicit and unspoken, regarding the effort required of the student (e.g. how many hours of work each week), what a student is permitted to work on, whether they even engage in research rather than serving a lab maintenance function, and how often they interact with the PI.

As our graduate and peer mentors prepare their students for these (often disagreeable) aspects of research, STEM AP students gain critical knowledge about how to identify the most appropriate research opportunities, learn to assess the lab environment, and begin to ask critical questions about what they will be permitted to do. Our students bring this self-confidence and knowledge to their research interviews and, thus armored, have a far higher chance of being chosen by the PIs. In fact, we now have a solid reputation for providing students who are self-confident, mature, and can hit the ground running. It is rare for any STEM AP student not to be chosen by a lab in their sophomore year if they wish to engage in research.

Rosie, a first-generation student who had recently joined STEM AP, reflected on the key role of her graduate mentors in preparing her to seek access to a research laboratory. "STEM AP was a great opportunity for me to learn even more from my graduate mentors as well as my peers. This past week, we went over elevator pitches and further looked into what kind of research, if any, that we would like to be involved in. It was a lot of fun and I think it will be very handy when I begin to apply to research labs and when I do other things as well, like apply to jobs in my field of interest, around the time I graduate from UMass Amherst." Rosie's experiences with mentoring are similar to those recounted by most of our early-career students. Having someone to turn to makes all the difference to these students as they attempt to integrate into the college experience.

Craig similarly reflected on how his self-confidence has grown through the mentoring experiences he has had in STEM AP. "Regarding STEM AP, I felt enough confidence to go to my professor's office hours and make a connection between him and I. Without the peer mentoring part of STEM AP, I don't think I would have built up enough courage to do so. Other than that, as a freshman, I've been trying to be more involved on campus and actually take initiative for my future career. I have applied to be a scribe at a local hospital and with this opportunity, I know I will gain much clinical experience. Though the shifts may be long and hard, my goal is to push through, no matter how much I may want to sleep in. I've also taken a note on which labs I would like to be a part of in the close future! All I have to do is send an email and I'm all set. With the grad mentors helping me, I know I'll be able to join the most interesting lab."

These mentoring sessions are not always highly focused and intense. Indeed, sometimes it is equally important for our students to simply enjoy each other's company. In this process, students gain the self-confidence to tackle the more stressful activities, such as choosing a research lab. Dan recalled how his mentoring session helped him simply enjoy his week. "During STEM AP, I met with my graduate mentors and we did a lot of very helpful activities. Everyone in my group showed them our resumes and they gave us advice on other things that we could put on our resumes, and helped us arrange them in a more logical, typical way. We also further discussed whether or not we wanted to join labs and just had a good time talking to one another. STEM AP was a great start to my week that allowed me to have a fun rest of the week."

Gisella, an experienced peer mentor, described her approach to lowering the stress so many of our students feel when considering if, when, and how to join a research lab. "During the peer mentoring session this week, I noticed that my mentees were stressed about finding a lab to join or were confused about whether or not they fit in their current lab. They asked me about my thoughts in determining whether their current lab was a good fit, and if was not, then how they can look for another lab. I shared my experience of looking for a lab in my sophomore year, and how I switched labs until I found the best fit for me in my senior year. In addition, I also discussed with them strategies to network and find different labs around campus, and then identify which lab's goal might be the best fit for them. This opportunity to become a peer mentor has allowed me to not only improve my leadership and communication skills, but it has also offered me a chance to help other students at UMass to approach their goals by sharing with them my experiences at UMass after almost four years. I really appreciate this opportunity!"

Our students instantly recognize the importance of their mentors in helping them achieve their goals, particularly with respect to gaining access to a research lab. Natalie's reflection on how her mentors helped her find the right research lab is similar to the experiences of many of our newest members. "Before meeting my mentors, Nidhi and Hailey, I had a goal of joining a lab. As a premed student, I knew that was one of the first things I wanted to do the second I started college, whether that be online or in person. After meeting Nidhi and Hailey, I was able to achieve that goal, as I am now working in a neurobiology lab! This lab was the first and only lab that I had taken a deep interest in after seeing the PI in a Netflix docuseries regarding the development of children. Knowing that I wanted to work with children in the future, I knew that this was the opportunity for me. When I finally got into the lab, I was beyond excited, and that could not have been possible without the help of my mentors."

Summer Research Experiences

The NSF has made a significant effort to incentivize STEM faculty to provide summer research experiences for undergraduates, particularly URM students. STEM AP adopted this practice from the start and thus offers five to eight research awards each year. Students are invited to apply for these grants and student leaders help the administrators identify the recipients. We place a significant emphasis on having our students articulate why they should be chosen for this opportunity and how it will impact their educational experience or help them reach their career goals.

Our graduate mentors often serve as research advisors to these summer students and prepare them ahead of time for what they will encounter. STEM AP also created a special summer support program to ensure our interns are constructively and happily engaged in their research. Students meet each week for lunch and discuss their experiences. Student leaders plan social events to get them out of their research labs for brief forays to amusement parks, beaches, movies, and the like, which helps transform an intense learning experience into one that also builds strong bonds between STEM AP members.

The success our students have in gaining transformative research experiences is truly inspiring. Many of our students, who often enter the program with the goal of attending medical school, end up enjoying their research so much that they choose to pursue graduate-level research over medical school. Further, they are highly competitive in obtaining travel funds to present their research at national undergraduate research conferences. Finally, they share these experiences with their peers in Monday night seminars and serve as role models and fountains of inspiration for our younger students. STEM AP provides direction along a research path that is often initially hidden from their view, helps them understand the power of a research experience in defining themselves as scientists, and offers them training in some of the basic skills required to compete for a research position. Once informed and trained, our students become the coveted prizes in research labs across campus that we always knew them to be!

References

1. Kitchen, J. A.; Sonnert, G.; Sadler, P. M. The Impact of College- and University-Run High School Summer Programs on Students' End of High School STEM Career Aspirations. *Sci. Educ.* **2018**, *102* (3), 529–547. DOI:10.1002/sce.21332.
2. Rodríguez Amaya, L.; Betancourt, T.; Collins, K. H.; Hinojosa, O.; Corona, C. Undergraduate Research Experiences: Mentoring, Awareness, and Perceptions—A Case Study at a Hispanic-Serving Institution. *Int. J. STEM Educ.* **2018**, *5* (1), 9. DOI:10.1186/s40594-018-0105-8.
3. Cooper, K. M.; Gin, L. E.; Akeeh, B.; Clark, C. E.; Hunter, J. S.; Roderick, T. B.; Elliott, D. B.; Gutierrez, L. A.; Mello, R. M.; Pfeiffer, L. D.; Scott, R. A.; Arellano, D.; Ramirez, D.; Valdez, E. M.; Vargas, C.; Velarde, K.; Zheng, Y.; Brownell, S. E. Factors That Predict Life Sciences Student Persistence in Undergraduate Research Experiences. *PLoS One* **2019**, *14* (8), e0220186. DOI:10.1371/journal.pone.0220186.
4. Hernandez, P. R.; Woodcock, A.; Estrada, M.; Schultz, P. W. Undergraduate Research Experiences Broaden Diversity in the Scientific Workforce. *BioScience* **2018**, *68* (3), 204–211. DOI:10.1093/biosci/bix163.
5. Rodenbusch, S. E.; Hernandez, P. R.; Simmons, S. L.; Dolan, E. L. Early Engagement in Course-Based Research Increases Graduation Rates and Completion of Science, Engineering,

and Mathematics Degrees. *CBE Life Sci. Educ.* **2016**, *15* (2), Ar.20. DOI:10.1187/cbe.16-03-0117.

6. *Research Experiences for Undergraduates (REU). Search for an REU Site.* https://www.nsf.gov/crssprgm/reu/reu_search.jsp
7. James, S. M.; Singer, S. R. From the NSF: The National Science Foundation's Investments in Broadening Participation in Science, Technology, Engineering, and Mathematics Education Through Research and Capacity Building. *CBE Life Sci. Educ.* **2016**, *15* (3). DOI:10.1187/cbe.16-01-0059.
8. Auchincloss, L. C.; Laursen, S. L.; Branchaw, J. L.; Eagan, K.; Graham, M.; Hanauer, D. I.; Lawrie, G.; McLinn, C. M.; Pelaez, N.; Rowland, S.; Towns, M.; Trautmann, N. M.; Varma-Nelson, P.; Weston, T. J.; Dolan, E. L. Assessment of Course-Based Undergraduate Research Experiences: A Meeting Report. *CBE Life Sci. Educ.* **2014**, *13* (1), 29–40. DOI:10.1187/cbe.14-01-0004.
9. Bakshi, A.; Patrick, L. E.; Wischusen, E. W. A Framework for Implementing Course-Based Undergraduate Research Experiences (CUREs) in Freshman Biology Labs. *Am. Biol. Teach.* **2016**, *78* (6), 448–455. DOI:10.1525/abt.2016.78.6.448.
10. Bangera, G.; Brownell, S. E. Course-Based Undergraduate Research Experiences Can Make Scientific Research More Inclusive. *CBE Life Sci. Educ.* **2014**, *13* (4), 602–606. DOI:10.1187/cbe.14-06-0099.
11. Indorf, J. L.; Weremijewicz, J.; Janos, D. P.; Gaines, M. S. Adding Authenticity to Inquiry in a First-Year, Research-Based, Biology Laboratory Course. *CBE Life Sci. Educ.* **2019**, *18* (3), Ar.38. DOI:10.1187/cbe.18-07-0126.
12. Gallego, M.; Busch, C. Preparing Teaching Assistants to Work With All Learners: The Impact of Accessibility Training. *Foreign Lang. Ann.* **2017**, *50* (4), 776–792. DOI:10.1111/flan.12305.
13. Freeman, S.; Eddy, S. L.; McDonough, M.; Smith, M. K.; Okoroafor, N.; Jordt, H.; Wenderoth, M. P. Active Learning Increases Student Performance in Science, Engineering, and Mathematics. *Proc. Natl. Acad. Sci. U. S. A.* **2014**, *111* (23), 8410–8415. DOI:10.1073/pnas.1319030111.
14. Borda, E.; Schumacher, E.; Hanley, D.; Geary, E.; Warren, S.; Ipsen, C.; Stredicke, L. Initial Implementation of Active Learning Strategies in Large, Lecture STEM Courses: Lessons Learned From a Multi-Institutional, Interdisciplinary STEM Faculty Development Program. *Int. J. S.T.E.M. Educ.* **2020**, *7* (1), 4. DOI:10.1186/s40594-020-0203-2.
15. Santore, C., Eds., *Aesop's Fables: The Classic Edition*, 1st ed.; Applesauce Press, Kennebunkport, ME, 2018.
16. Dolan, E.; Micklos, D.; Trautmann, N. CURE *Collection*, 2020. https://serc.carleton.edu/curenet/index.html
17. Ballen, C. J.; Blum, J. E.; Brownell, S.; Hebert, S.; Hewlett, J.; Klein, J. R.; McDonald, E. A.; Monti, D. L.; Nold, S. C.; Slemmons, K. E.; Soneral, P. A. G.; Cotner, S. A Call to Develop Course-Based Undergraduate Research Experiences (CUREs) for Nonmajors Courses. *CBE Life Sci. Educ.* **2017**, *16* (2). DOI:10.1187/cbe.16-12-0352.
18. Ing, M.; Burnette, J. M.; Azzam, T.; Wessler, S. R. Participation in a Course-Based Undergraduate Research Experience Results in Higher Grades in the Companion Lecture Course. *Educ. Res.* **2021**, *50* (4), 205–214. DOI:10.3102/0013189X20968097.
19. Estrada, M.; Burnett, M.; Campbell, A. G.; Campbell, P. B.; Denetclaw, W. F.; Gutiérrez, C. G.; Hurtado, S.; John, G. H.; Matsui, J.; McGee, R.; Okpodu, C. M.; Robinson, T. J.; Summers, M. F.; Werner-Washburne, M.; Zavala, M. Improving Underrepresented Minority Student Persistence in STEM. *CBE Life Sci. Educ.* **2016**, *15* (3). DOI:10.1187/cbe.16-01-0038.

20. Heim, A. B.; Holt, E. A. Benefits and Challenges of Instructing Introductory Biology Course-Based Undergraduate Research Experiences (CUREs) as Perceived by Graduate Teaching Assistants. *CBE Life Sci. Educ.* **2019**, *18* (3), Ar.43. DOI:10.1187/cbe.18-09-0193.
21. Delventhal, R.; Steinhauer, J. A Course-Based Undergraduate Research Experience Examining Neurodegeneration in *Drosophila melanogaster* Teaches Students to Think, Communicate, and Perform Like Scientists. *PLoS One* **2020**, *15* (4), e0230912. DOI:10.1371/journal.pone.0230912.
22. Mendoza, N.; Richard, J.; Wickliff, T. *Enculturation of Diverse Students to the Engineering Sciences Through First Year Engineering Experiences at a Southwestern Institution: An Exploratory Work in Progress*; Roanoke, VA, 2015. The 123rd American Society for Engineering Education (ASEE) Annual Conference and Exposition, New Orleans, LA: USA. Project: NSF-RIEF: Engineering Enculturation of the First-Year Engineering Students.
23. Shortlidge, E. E.; Bangera, G.; Brownell, S. E. Each to Their Own CURE: Faculty Who Teach Course-Based Undergraduate Research Experiences Report Why You Too Should Teach a CURE. *J. Microbiol. Biol. Educ.* **2017**, *18* (2). DOI:10.1128/jmbe.v18i2.1260.
24. McMurtrie, B. Many Professors Want to Change Their Teaching but Don't. One University Found Out Why. *The Chronicle for Higher Education.* March 21, 2019.
25. Staub, N. L.; Poxleitner, M.; Braley, A.; Smith-Flores, H.; Pribbenow, C. M.; Jaworski, L.; Lopatto, D.; Anders, K. R. Scaling Up: Adapting a Phage-Hunting Course to Increase Participation of First-Year Students in Research. *CBE Life Sci. Educ.* **2016**, *15* (2), Ar.13. DOI:10.1187/cbe.15-10-0211.

Chapter 5

The Power of a Community to Transform STEM Students

Monday Night Seminar

It is Monday night and our students have started to converge within our gathering space, a large classroom furnished with round tables that comfortably seat 10. Students come here from all over campus, streaming through several entrances to the building from multiple directions. They walk purposefully through the corridors, anxious to arrive. The huge room quickly fills; students walk across it to greet each other. The space is soon abuzz with the murmur of friendly conversation; sometimes, the steady hum is interrupted by peals of laughter. Soon, the room is called to attention by one of the program directors or student leaders. Silence ensues. It is time to begin. The STEM AP Monday night seminar is underway!

First-generation college students, those who are Pell Grant eligible, and other underrepresented minorities, fill the seats and look on in anticipation. It is an unusual room because the bodies in it represent students who disproportionately drop out of STEM. This is an ever-present reminder of why our program exists at all. Here, in this room, lies our response to the enduring problem of the lack of diversity in STEM. It is not simply about the practical solution: providing all the resources our students will need to excel in STEM. Here, we allow them to exist in a space and context that sanctions who they are, that pays attention to their needs.

These two features of our solution overlap; among the most overlooked resources in STEM are the people who do science. The power of community to influence STEM learning was expressed by one of our second-year students who had some uncertainty about how to get into a lab: "During the STEM AP seminar, I learned more information about how to be in a research lab and just more general information about what it takes to be in a lab. In the group that we were in, some had research experience and others didn't; I was one of the people that didn't. I have been looking into different labs but don't really know how to go about the process of approaching them. I got really good advice about how to go about and start the process of getting into research."

To tell it and to experience it are totally different things. The magic of the STEM AP seminar space is very much like a marketplace that vibrates with idea

Empowering Underrepresented Students in Science. DOI: http://dx.doi.org/10.1016/B978-0-323-90469-8.00005-6

and activity exchange each Monday night. Students learn about the research of scholars from all aspects of STEM. They interact with these researchers and each other around the issues presented; they engage in near-peer mentoring; they develop critical skills; and they socialize. It is a particularly empowering opportunity for the older students to give back to their peers based on their personal experiences of being STEM scholars. Student leaders conduct training that supports the mentoring practices of the peer mentors. Graduate students mentor first-year students, introducing them to their own research topics while helping them read and understand scholarly articles. Second-year students receive training and support to prepare their resumes for internship applications and learn how to create and present elevator pitches that express their areas of study and research, as well as their goals for the future. Upper-year students help each other prepare for GRE, MCAT, and DAT tests, sessions which they organize and coordinate on their own. Seniors also are afforded time to prepare presentations for the entire group that focus on their accomplishments in research, internships, travels, and work.

Students form close relationships with each other and also get to interact with graduate mentors, student leaders, and program administrators. It is no wonder that students find these sessions robust, rich, and immersive. They walk away from meaningful interactions each week, hopefully more empowered, confident, and clear-eyed about the direction they intend to pursue in their career path. At the very least, for those students harboring lingering doubts or facing ongoing struggles, we strive to reassure them that they have a community with rich resources to which they can look to, for the needed help and support.

Lana tells this story better than we can, and her experiences and feelings are shared by many of our younger students. "I am so excited to be a part of the STEM Ambassadors Program for another semester. I learned a great deal from the experiences that this program has to offer, and I am looking forward to this opportunity again" she explained. "The first two seminars have already been very helpful and have opened my eyes to various possibilities. Last week, I enjoyed meeting with my new peer mentor and learning about how to adjust to my new classes. Upon entering the new semester, I was very nervous about my new classes. I did not realize that the workload for each class would increase significantly. This is something I needed to adjust to quickly. Although I was overwhelmed, my peer mentor was able to help ease my mind and remind me that this semester will only be what I make of it."

The perspective provided by one of our more experienced STEM Ambassadors, Amber, is equally revealing. "My past years with STEM AP have allowed me to be part of such an amazing group where I feel included and learn so much from those around me. Although it is coming to an end, class-wise, I know STEM will still be a part of my life, as well as everyone else's."

And finally, Arshia reflected: "This whole semester, I struggled a lot with purpose and destiny. I believe it's time for me to sit back and realize the amazing things I've gone through these last few months and the places I will go.

I'm extremely ready for a break, like anybody else, and I will truly miss STEM AP over the winter break. I am so happy that I have found such an amazing program to be involved in, and I am so happy to be able to be immersed in such a positive learning environment with like-minded people. It is amazing to hear some of the things that my peers have done and are doing, and that inspires me more to work harder and get better for a successful future, like everyone in STEM AP."

The community we strive to create and maintain relies heavily on the support that students derive from the help and leadership of their peers. As mentioned throughout this text, mentoring plays a crucial role at all levels of this program. The sense of empowerment and affirmation students derive from mentoring and/or being mentored by their peers in this intimate community cannot be overstated. Darren says it best in his reflection on STEM AP: "I have to say that my favorite thing about STEM AP is the connections that I get to make with other students in STEM. During this near-peer mentoring meeting, all of us talked about the classes we plan on taking next semester and the challenges we see ourselves facing. If it was not for the constant support I experience from STEM AP, I definitely would be a lot more stressed about school!"

Arshia came to a similar conclusion in one of her reflections. "Recently I've been struggling with whether this is what I am meant to do and if this is my purpose in life. It's almost a sense of impostor syndrome that I experience. Occasionally, I don't feel like I am meant to be where I am today, but I am very thankful to be here. I have a feeling that I will feel the same way throughout my process to becoming a physician! It was nice to hear the guest speaker's experiences on working and application process, which causes me a lot of worry. Every week, I am more and more thankful that I'm in STEM AP because it provides me with a sense of community, [of being] around similar-minded people. It brings me much hope for the future and confidence that I can get through my struggles."

We Must Be Deliberate

STEM spaces are generally found to be competitive, individualistic, objective, and somewhat cold.[1] Indeed, the dominant culture in STEM has privileged norms of success that favor competitive, individualistic, and solitary practices—norms typically associated with white male scientists.[2] This privilege extends to learning practices in STEM education that have marginalized groups not conventionally associated with mainstream STEM success.[2] The students, researchers, and professionals who occupy these spaces understand that they are not usually sites of socialization or warmth, which is why, in part, so many STEM students find their classrooms and research labs intimidating, stress-filled, and lonely. Such students are frequently pushed out of STEM due to negative experiences within science spaces, where many are marginalized and their interests suppressed.[3] These students—who are the heart of STEM

AP—struggle to find their place, and these struggles often lead them to seek out or create counterspaces.[2] In this very real sense, the STEM AP's approach to providing support to our students runs counter to the general culture of STEM. It provides a STEM counterspace that is warm and inviting: a community in every sense of the word. In it, we teach collaboration by being collaborative; we teach warmth and the value of the presence of each member of the community by being warm and welcoming.

Mei-Li reflected on the key role STEM AP has played in her own emotional development as a student. "The weekly STEM AP meetings were a regular reminder that I am not on my own in the pursuit of my STEM major. When I am placed in a situation where I am extremely stressed with work and on the verge of a burnout, knowing that so many of my peers are in the same boat gives me a sense of relief. The near-peer mentoring sessions enabled me to catch up with my mentees while also giving me the opportunity to feel good about the accomplishments I made that past week, given that I was in my mentee's shoes just a year ago. Now that I am advising others, it allows me to reflect on myself and realize how far I have come, which I find to be very motivating in my future endeavors."

Sabba focused on the role STEM AP serves in providing a calming touchstone each week. "This week, I am looking forward to the STEM AP lecture and the peer mentoring groups; I have been really busy this semester because I am taking more classes than I should have, but the STEM AP classes are refreshing and interactive, which is [very] different from most of my other classes. It is nice to be able to talk about the stress of the semester with other students in STEM AP, especially since we no longer have the opportunity to do it in person. I also look forward to the sophomore peer group on professional development because I do feel like I am lacking in extracurricular activities, and being off campus makes it harder to find opportunities to build my resume."

Finally, Dinh spoke to the importance of having access to the wealth of knowledge provided by our Monday night program "This week's guest lecture was probably my favorite so far. I have been going back and forth about my pre-med path, and whether or not it is something I truly want/am prepared to embark on. I think it was very informative and reassuring to have someone in med school talk about all the challenges she faced, and to be so open and honest about her mental health and experiences within med school. I really appreciated her constant reassurance, and the faith that she had in all of us and our journey. I think along the way, it is very easy to begin to doubt yourself, and not see your full potential. Knowing that there are others who experience the same things you do, is very comforting; to know that you are not alone. It also gives you the opportunity to reevaluate your strengths and weaknesses, and realize you are simply being too hard on yourself. This week's discussion definitely gave a perception of med school that I needed, because there is no one else in my life that has gone through med school that I can talk to about my process, or feelings, so having this opportunity to hear from our guest lecturer was something I truly appreciated, and since then, I have been putting in more thought about what I want for my future."

Another student, Asiah, reflected on that same session: "This week in my discussion group, we discussed many different things that helped us want to be in medicine. It was quite eye-opening to be able to draw from my own personal struggles and experiences that have made me want to go into medicine. It was very nice to listen to my fellow peers when discussing their experiences, that made them want to pursue medicine. I truly love being involved in a community that it just like me and loves medicine as much as I do!"

Meanwhile, yet another student benefited in a completely different way from the same session. Ariana remarked on how the program is broadening her perspective about the diversity of interests among her peers. "I enjoyed the guest lecture a lot this week. I didn't really know anything about medical school because I don't intend to go to it, but it was neat to hear about the speaker's life and how STEM AP helped her. It's interesting being in a STEM club because being in pure math (which I wouldn't really consider STEM) feels so different from what everyone else does, and it's cool to learn about all the neat things my peers are doing."

If we ask why community matters so much in increasing STEM retention, one answer quickly comes into focus: our students need the support, mentorship, and inspiration only they can provide each other. Their presence in STEM classrooms and labs encourages the presence and persistence of other students with similar backgrounds, motivating them to join and to stay in STEM. The community of STEM scholars that we build is powerful. Not only is it a community that seeks to give, but it is a community that demands from its members much of the richness of what they bring and are able to offer. It empowers them as scientists who are not only required to excel in their academic contexts, but to excel in social contexts as they exchange who they are with their colleagues, both those with similar backgrounds and experiences and those who are very different from themselves.

Luna commented on precisely this aspect of the STEM AP community in one of her reflections. "I am so grateful to STEM AP for creating such a supportive community and a motivating environment for me and everyone. STEM AP not only helped me in my academic experience at UMass but it's helped me become more comfortable with who I am. I've grown up in many places; most of them were predominantly white and conservative communities, and I am south Asian. This made it difficult for me to fully embrace my cultural background and heritage. Coming to STEM AP and seeing so many minority students succeed in this field and in their college careers has been such an empowering and motivating experience. It has taught me to appreciate my differences. Even though I haven't utilized all the resources available in STEM AP, I love this program and it's had more of an impact on my life than probably any other organization I've been a part of. I am excited to see what's to come for STEM AP and I hope that we find ways to continue to make this program available to students, because it has such a tremendously positive impact on everyone that's a part of it."

At this point, we must note a critical distinction between STEM AP and many other STEM retention programs. Our program is about the community, for the community, and by the community. We bring all our resources, activities, and socializing into a structured, predictable community event: Monday night seminars. Students in STEM AP are mentored, just as many other programs provide mentoring. However, in STEM AP, that mentoring is set within a context of a room filled with like-minded people sharing similar struggles and challenges. This truly does make all the difference. Students create a living, breathing entity—the STEM AP community—that becomes their touchstone throughout their college experience.

That is what Luna referred to in her reflection above and what Darshana also notes: "I am going to reflect on my entire semester on STEM AP in this reflection. For starters, when I joined STEM AP, I had no idea what it was. I joined it because I got the email and it was one way to get involved. Little did I know that I would become so invested in the program. I made sure I showed up every week and actually listened to the guest lecture, and I made sure that I talked with my peer advisor. However, the most helpful thing I found was the graduate advisors, because they helped me formulate emails to send out to PIs to get into research labs. Overall, joining the STEM AP program was very helpful for me to feel welcome in the UMass community."

Tristram provides a delightful description of the STEM AP community in his reflection. "I cannot believe I am done with my first college semester. With the complications that came with being remote and not having that realistic college experience, I still managed to enjoy it and learn more than I expected. One of the classes I wished I could have attended in-person is STEM AP. I still remember the first meeting of the semester. It was filled with enthusiasm and [a feeling of] community! It was a class I would have loved because I love making new friends! It was a way to collaborate with individuals who hold the same interests and can build a successful community. Although it was remote, that sense of community was still there between students in breakout rooms. Even my mentors were filled with happiness and guidance. Overall, it was a great experience." Even though Tristram was not able to be present in the same room as his peers, he felt what all of our students feel: STEM AP is theirs; it is warm and it is filled with "happiness and guidance."

The STEM AP is a different kind of STEM space; in fact, it is actually a STEM counterspace.[2] And this is important for our students to understand. It presents an alternative to the "norm." It is in this collaborative community of scientists that we enable our students to pursue research opportunities, to approach research scientists for much-needed guidance, training, and feedback, and to go after Summer REUs or apply to medical school, graduate programs, or for employment. Our students are bolstered by the fact that they have friends who have excelled in classes in which they may be currently struggling, or who hold positions of leadership in other contexts across campus and are able to advise them as they pursue similar interests. Students have friends with whom they meet for lunch, or coffee or to work out with or catch a movie. Friends introduce their friends and expand their closest circles.

So why a STEM community, you ask? The benefits are endless. And as varied and intertwining as they can be, as you've seen in this chapter, there is yet much more that our STEM community has offered to the students who are its members and co-creators.

Natasha remarked on the importance of the STEM AP community in one of her reflections. "Last week, we had our first STEM AP meeting of the spring semester and it was great to see everyone return. I felt like I have started to develop new friendships and bonds with my peers from the STEM AP community. After last week's seminar, I made the decision to be more present and get more involved in STEM AP and contribute in the best way that I can, which I am certain will have a positive impact on my experience as a freshman here at UMass and as a STEM major. There are many aspects and principles of STEM AP that align with some of the goals that I have set for myself for this upcoming semester and year, such as diversity, acceptance, and networking. These are valuable skills and characteristics to have as a person, especially in such a competitive and extensive field. By getting more involved in the STEM AP community, I hope to develop and sharpen these skills through daily interactions with my peers and the supervisors."

Arielle also reflected on the importance of the STEM AP community, particularly in helping her step outside her comfort zone. "The most significant STEM-related activity I did this week is attend career fairs. I think a lot of what I learned about community building and engagement applied to these career fairs. I remember constructing my elevator pitch in sophomore-level programming and it feels so good to be able to apply that skill and try and find a job. STEM AP has taught me to step out of my comfort zone and try new things. That's why I'm applying to biotech companies and pharmaceutical companies, to expand my horizons. I feel much more comfortable facing the future with these skills and confidence."

In a similar vein, Alfonzo wrote about the importance of the STEM AP community in fostering his professional growth. "This past week at STEM AP, I got phenomenal advice from my two peer advisors. I got some great advice about taking research opportunities and getting volunteering opportunities. I was enlightened to the idea of asking my cousins, who work at hospitals, to try to get me volunteer service this summer. The experience would look fantastic on my resume and get me a base of knowledge that would help me compete against other people in future opportunities. One of them was even happy enough to look at my old high school resume and help me revise it for the future, to be more fitting for college. Other than that, we just talked about life and college in general, and they are really helping me feel more comfortable for the future because I know I have two people I can turn to for any questions!"

In addition to the crucial role the STEM AP community plays in the personal growth of our students, it also fulfills another fairly basic need:

providing them with their own personal networking system. As potential outsiders to the dominant STEM spaces on campus, our students often fail to integrate into the powerful networking opportunities that exist in most departments; in fact, they rarely even realize that such resources exist. If they don't attend departmental seminar series, strike up relationships with their professors, or get invited to serve as an undergraduate teaching assistant, they may miss out on making valuable professional connections. Cecelia spoke to the role STEM AP serves in this regard. "One of the most beneficial and important characteristics of STEM AP is that it is a network of information. We, as a group, are filled with a diverse range of people that are exposed to a diverse range of information. When we gather together during our Monday night seminars, we put all of our information together. This allows for people to discover opportunities, programs, and more that they, under normal circumstances, would have never heard of before."

One of the most common reflections that we read from our first-year students is exemplified through the words of Lava, a self-proclaimed overachiever majoring in mathematics. "There was another math club meeting this week and I saw Henry and Chengzhi from my STEM AP near-peer mentoring group there, which was nice. We are very friendly and it is nice to have some connections. For such a large school, it is really incredible how small the math department feels (and STEM AP). Everyone remembers me and is super nice. For all of the hard things that are happening right now, I really couldn't have asked for a better online learning experience. I hope that I can make some more friends and connections through STEM AP because the people I have met so far have been some of the kindest people I have ever met." Lava cares deeply about his STEM AP community because it is warm, welcoming, and personal. STEM AP provides a home away from home for many of our students, and this comfort translates into higher levels of self-confidence and an increased sense of self— precisely what our students want and need to survive in the challenging world of STEM studies.

The STEM AP Office

Our office is staffed by undergraduate students who have been interviewed, chosen, and trained for positions of responsibility. We try to ensure that the office reflects our ethos, providing a warm and welcoming space for all. There is a long table in the middle of the fairly large space. It seats six comfortably but has the capacity to seat many more. On many occasions, it has had to! This table is the centerpiece of our STEM community space. Students come to study, meet, tutor, mentor, eat, or just to enjoy the safety of a space that affirms and welcomes their presence.

This is the physical heart of our community. It often becomes overcrowded, especially on days when mentors gather for the prep session before they go off to the rooms designated for middle school mentoring. In this room that exists to support their presence and aspirations, students feel safe enough to be vulnerable and to speak the unspeakable: their struggles in class, their personal struggles, their uncertainty about plans for their chosen professional paths and plans for their future lives in general. They listen, they support, they give advice, they discuss, they disagree, they laugh, they chat (sometimes too loudly), they commune, and, not infrequently, they cry.

Our effort to provide such a space for just such a purpose is significant. The atmosphere the administrators and student workers engender is deliberately crafted. The vision of our program is to be an *inclusive* community, a community that welcomes ALL of its members with open arms. Once you are invited to be a part of STEM AP, we do all we can to embrace you as a whole person. That is what a community ought to be: welcoming, inviting, inspiring, and affirming.

There are times when students need the quiet confidentiality of a private conference with an administrator, and perhaps even their intervention and advocacy in a situation that warrants it. We have done this time and again on behalf of our students. We are always aware that the role our program plays must be clear and constant. Only consistency can ensure that our students experience an authentic sense of confidence and security, knowing that they are truly valued and supported.

As Nora explained, "This week I started going to the STEM AP office to do my homework. This has contributed to my personal STEM development because I am able to communicate with other STEM majors and learn about possible upper-level biology classes and about opportunities available to STEM majors. On Monday, I learned about the research and lab opportunities offered at the school, which I will be applying for."

Emily, meanwhile, addressed a more personal and intimate role that the office has served. In this case, the person sitting in the office provided the key: "If the director is reading this, I can only hope to say how grateful I am to have had three meaningful years to learn from you as a student. I am incredibly grateful for the amount of time you spent with me while I was convinced that the sky was burning down. I can only hope to pay it forward and try to reach out to the next generation of STEM students and help them feel safe in the same way that STEM AP and you made me feel. I hope she realizes that she inspired a whole generation of scientists to avoid the toxicity of STEM and build each other up. From the bottom of my heart, I sincerely thank you."

The secret to the success of our STEM community space is that those who are the creators and leaders of the community must actually believe in the values and the philosophy that drive the community. The community leaders must be committed to inclusive pedagogy and seek to make it a way of life for all the members it serves. There can be no real change within STEM as a discipline if its leaders are not committed to the idea of inclusivity.[4] To this end, we support the aspirations of all students who want to develop as leaders. We provide numerous opportunities for them to gain leadership training and experience, and it is a frequent topic in our Monday night seminars. Anastasia reflected on the importance of leadership, saying: "This week during STEM AP, we talked about what it takes to become a leader. An important aspect of being a part of STEM AP is being able to be a leader and helping others. In the meeting, we focused on what attributes contribute to someone being a leader. In the end, [we] came to the conclusion that anything that involves you taking action and helping others can make you a leader. We even talked about why it's important to figure out what you're a leader in, because it can help you find characteristics to describe yourself when it comes to interviews. We also talked about the different opportunities at UMass that actually provide students with the opportunity to lead and help others."

Arshia found one leadership discussion particularly motivating. "This past STEM AP seminar, we had our class-level program, and it is always helpful to hear from students with more experience than me. This week, they talked about getting involved in leadership positions and different opportunities that UMass has to offer. I really want to get more involved in STEM AP to help a community that has helped me so much and to learn more about leadership."

In one of her reflections, Darshana, also commented on the importance of learning about leadership. "Last week, we had a great discussion on involvement and being an active community member, in any sort of community. One of the main characteristics that we associate with good community members is leadership. Being able to be a good leader and knowing what it takes to lead a group of individuals is very important. We can all be leaders, great leaders. We are all involved in activities, with family, friends, at school, or at work, through which we can showcase our leadership, to help and influence others. No initiative is too small, and no work is insignificant. This was something we touched upon in the last discussion on Monday that I hope to carry with me as I continue to be engaged in different activities, and look for ways to be an active member in my many communities."

Finally, Wei-Li described how this session helped her realize that she was already a leader. "This week went well in my breakout group. We talked about the different qualities of a leader and in what ways you can be a leader. I did not realize that I am actually more of a leader than I thought I was (peer mentor, TA, an officer in a club). Moreover, I talked with two STEM AP leaders about their positions and possibly taking over one of their roles! I am super excited to hopefully become a leader in STEM AP because I want to play a bigger role in the class and give back to my future STEM AP peers."

Our student leaders take their roles quite seriously. They meet each week to discuss programming matters, challenges that need to be addressed, and even who will man the office. The thought they put into their roles as leaders never ceases to amaze us. As one fairly new STEM AP leader put it while preparing for a Monday night programming presentation: "This week, I have been working on my presentation for STEM by discovering key points that not everyone is aware of. This includes finding the right 401(k), mortgages, finding the right apartment, and even how to stay organized in college. I will not go so deep into each topic to prevent overwhelming students, but I will be able to provide sufficient information that will allow them to still be informed. I want to be able to show the students that adulting may look scary, but it is truly a bunch of words that just need to be simplified. I hope to reach out to the audience and give them information they never knew they needed. This could include finding ways to manage school and life priorities."

The STEM AP office is more than simply a place to run the administrative functions of the program; more importantly, it provides shelter for our students. The connection they experience from being there with each other and the administrators contributes to their overall sense of belonging. These outcomes may appear to be merely coincidental benefits of a program that has an office location. After all, which program does not engender connection when members come frequently to its designated gathering spot? The difference with our STEM office, however, is in our deliberate investment in making the program's headquarters all that we promise our students it will be.[2] Research has shown that a welcoming office culture enables students to be candid about their struggles; it encourages honest talk, and it values and relies on the shared experiences of those present to creatively problem-solve with their peers.[5] Around our conference table, which is the center of the room and the beating heart of the office, are conversations that are fun and funny, as well as those that are reflective, that delve into the background stories of our students. Sometimes the conversations are not conducted in English; instead, Spanish, Igbo, French, Haitian Creole, or Vietnamese rings out. The STEM office affords students the freedom to be fully themselves without the need to "fix" who they are to fit in. It allows them to wholly embrace the scientific and non-scientific parts of their identities.[6]

Graduate mentors often stop in for brief chats, to tutor, or just to sit and be present. Colleagues of the program administrators stop in for social calls or to discuss work-related collaborations and to informally inform students of STEM-related college-sponsored events and initiatives. Very often, students get to chat informally with their professors as they pass by. Some visitors pop their heads in as they walk by, curious about a room that always seems to be pulsing with life and activity, and where laughter abounds. The STEM AP office gives context to our existence. Moreover, students learn to dispense with their anxieties and just be. The room has become known for its unconventional warmth and welcoming atmosphere, and it attracts the attention of many who would not normally initiate social interactions outside a cursory nod of acknowledgment (if that) as they go about their day. Admittedly, not all members of our program make it to the STEM AP office, certainly not on a regular basis, but a sense of security comes from knowing that the office is there, teeming with peers and others who stand ready to be a source of support when they need it. Each week at seminar, students are encouraged to pop in, if only to have lunch with others who are there.

The STEM AP office also provides a quiet study space for those who desire a spot other than the library or a regular classroom. Students take ownership of the room because it is theirs and it exists for their exclusive use. They often use the room for solo or group study. It is safe, it is available, and it is *theirs*. The room is equipped with computers salvaged from upgrades conducted in other offices in the building. They may not be the best, but we make them work and they augment the resources we try to make available for our students. We point this out as a way to note that you can do a lot with a little. Although we would advocate for allocating the best resources available at any institution with the will to create a similar space for its underrepresented STEM students, there are ways to make things work on a tight budget. However, what is more pressing is that such a space is created in the first place. The greatest advantage of having such a place is what the bodies that occupy it, do to make it inclusive and authentically welcoming and affirming for all who enter it.

This is how April described the office experience: "This week, I went to the STEM AP office to talk with the director about personal issues, school-related stress, and if I wanted to continue to apply to more REUs. After some open conversation about my mental and emotional drain and fatigue, the director suggested that I do what's best for my well-being by prioritizing what mattered to me. Being able to talk to the director at the STEM AP office and knowing that I have mentors to go to within the STEM field really reassures me and I'm happy I can come to them for guidance."

STEM AP and COVID-19

It was late February 2020 and we were hearing increasing accounts in the news of a virus that seemed to have taken hold of more and more communities across the nation and, indeed, the world. As a consequence, several US-based academic conferences sent cancellation announcements. Many of our students, who had been accepted to present at some of these conferences, expressed their disappointment and frustration at having these experiences delayed or possibly cancelled altogether.

Then came the most impactful announcement of all our own campus would close the very next day until some undetermined future time. The novel coronavirus pandemic had landed with a thud that reverberated throughout the land. Terms like "social distancing" and "mask wearing" and "hand washing" became our new vocabulary as we were, of necessity, ushered into the age of COVID-19.

This new normal naturally affected the running of our program. Classes had gone remote overnight. The concept was challenging for both students and their instructors, who had to turn their classes, specifically designed for in-person instruction, into virtual experiences. STEM AP was no exception. Our program had to move fast to transform its design so we could continue to provide support for our students, who had gone home for spring break but were now not allowed to return to campus, to complete the semester.

How did we do this? There was so much to take into consideration. The age of COVID-19 presented dramatic challenges for all concerned. For one, at the outset, we found the situation to be intensely disruptive, especially for an initiative based on community and togetherness. Our students were suddenly isolated from each other. Our office, our home space, was closed, along with the rest of the campus. Our marketplace-like meeting spot for weekly seminar came to an abrupt end. These conditions forced us to create a remote community literally overnight.

The importance of creating a remote version of STEM AP quickly became apparent. A fairly new member of STEM AP, Wei-Li, who joined us from China, reflected on the critical nature of having a supportive community to turn to during the pandemic. "STEM AP during COVID has helped me this week by allowing me to hear the experiences of those I consider role models and by answering questions that I may have had. I love how there is a space every Monday to get to know my peers because maintaining friends has been very hard this semester. I love how we got to talk about our week and are encouraged by those who understand our fears and how high our goals are. I am glad to have a conversation every week with others who also have goals and fears like mine, who understand how important they are."

Another student, Carlos, who self-identifies as a first-generation college student, remarked how the STEM AP community helped him feel understood. "This week, we went over how to deal with stress when it came to classes, especially online learning during the COVID-19 pandemic. I really liked how I could relate to other peers regarding first-generational issues while being at home. One example that I actually mentioned was my parents asking me to do chores and other tasks while I was in school. What seems to them to be spending hours on the computer doing nothing is actually me doing online school. It is hard for them to understand that. A few of my peers mentioned they could relate to me. I also just want to say that I really love the STEM AP community. I always look forward to the class because it allows me to de-stress a little and talk to some great people who are also in STEM."

Our students flocked to the remote community just as eagerly as they did to our in-person version. This was particularly important because many—perhaps most—of our students happen to be from some of the most vulnerable backgrounds and demographics in STEM. Though COVID-19 immediately impacted students across the country, students of color, minority students, and those from low-income backgrounds and unstable living situations were the worst affected, and the vast majority of our students so identify. Further, many of our students had been sent home to countries that had far fewer resources to ensure safety in the midst of the pandemic. Our students were isolated and alone, and STEM AP became a touchstone they turned to so they could remain connected.

Minh Quan accounted for this in one of his reflections. "I have learned a lot during the semester, and as a freshman international student, it has been the class where I was exposed to the most opportunities on campus and outside. I am really glad I am able to be part of this community. STEM AP is better in person, but continuing to have seminars every Monday is really amazing. It made me feel that sense of community even though we're all far away from each other."

Liz noted similar feelings in her final reflection from the fall of 2020: "Because this is the last reflection of the semester, I just want to personally thank everyone for their dedication and help throughout these past 13 weeks. STEM AP has helped me persevere through this semester, and it has given me something to look forward to every Monday. I truly enjoyed and appreciated all of the time and effort that were put into making this semester successful. With the given circumstances, all of the seminars went incredibly well, and I learned so much from the guest speakers. I wish you all the best and hope to see you soon."

A Community Is a Community Is a Community

The novel coronavirus was well on its deadly way by the time our community reconvened. We reworked and redesigned a program that could work virtually. We gathered our STEM Ambassadors together and offered community support remotely. We met, as student leaders and program administrators, to figure out the most meaningful way to offer support. Students were stressed. Doing schoolwork from home while adhering to newly imposed social distancing rules felt strange and artificial. It was spring. The sun was out. The days were consistently getting brighter. The trees and flowers were budding and it was noticeably warmer, but being out and about socializing with friends or sun worshiping would not be the norm in 2020. The strange time demanded we find ways to cope.

And so it was that STEM AP entered into the remote phase of its programming. When word came that classes would not be renewed in person, we quickly created a program that would accommodate our students in an online format. The nucleus of the story is that our focus remained: We are a community that provides support and allows its members to offer service and support to each other, and we would continue to do just that in whatever format we could, in person or remotely. We have continued as a virtual community since the COVID-19-imposed shutdown of normal campus operations. We recruited new students for the following fall semester, and those students, mostly first-year students just entering college, came out of their need to find connection and support.

As classes began at the start of the fall semester, we were delighted to welcome a new and enthusiastic batch of freshmen and upperclassmen who had heard of our program and registered for it. Naturally, we had never had the privilege of planning an entire semester of activities in this format before. Indeed, it was exciting to have students check in through our online system from all over the United States and abroad. Our students hail from Nigeria, China, India, Spain, Haiti, and many other countries, reaffirming the great diversity of our community. These were students who could not physically come to the university. They were being introduced to college life from the isolated space of their individual countries and in their individual homes, separated from friends and family members because of the imposition of social distancing. It was under these circumstances that we offered community to our diverse constituents.

The remote community our program created out of necessity acted as a haven for students who would otherwise have felt even more intensely displaced by having to acclimate to college life without the benefit of a circle of peers with whom to bond and collaborate. Students who connected virtually each week spoke of the sense of connection they experienced, even though they were miles apart. As long as students experience the sense of connection and support we have advanced throughout this text, our program is serving them well. Even in a virtual context, providing space for students to get together and learn together, and be a presence and resource for each other is crucial. In line with the provisions of our program, students found it tremendously beneficial to their morale, their self-efficacy, and their budding science identities. Our students, especially our newest members who have not had the opportunity of experiencing the community face-to-face, were nonetheless gratified they had our group of STEM scholars to turn to during what was a bewildering start, on many levels, to their college careers. Having the support of upper-level peers as well as the encouragement and guidance of graduate mentors, went a long way in allowing our students to experience what being part of a community was all about. We maintain that the creation of a virtual space filled a crucial gap at a time when there was dire need for it.

One of our most devoted seniors, Mai Pho, spoke of the key role STEM AP served during this remote learning period. "Although I haven't been able to attend the seminars in real time, the STEM AP community has allowed me to connect with peers and seniors and made me feel like part of the UMass community during this virtual semester. Each week, I have been introduced to a new concept and heard so many wonderful people speak about their contributions. It has really inspired me to be a better and more active person in the community. Really looking forward to the last stretch of this semester."

Another senior, Rosella, reflected on the key role STEM AP has played in helping her remain connected with the university during the pandemic. "This week in STEM AP, we met in our peer mentoring groups. In my group, we talked about how the semester was going so far for each of us. My semester so far hasn't gone as I was imagining it would go. I didn't realize how difficult the easiest things would be, because everything is remote. Now it takes me all day to do work that would normally have taken one or two hours. This might be because for most of my classes, I am having to teach everything to myself and it is really hard to get help because most of my time is being consumed by other classes or work. In my small group, we also talked about our future plans and ambitions/goals. It was really great to hear others speak of their experiences about this semester because I feel really isolated, being away from friends and being so far from campus. Talking to others and relating to them helps me feel understood and [gives me] a sense of community."

A first-semester freshman, Cecilia reminded us that STEM AP also provides something less intense: a place to explore options, connect with peers, and be happy! "In the home stretch of my first semester in college, everything is stressful but I think it's going well. STEM AP on Monday had the presentation by Ranjana about med school and that was so cool! Personally, I wasn't thinking about going to med school or pursuing the pre-med track, but after that presentation, I might be showing some interest. I'm not sure, though; but I still have some time to decide what I want to do. We also met with our graduate mentors again, which was great! I got the week wrong, so I was pleasantly surprised when I saw that they were joining us this week. We had a no-dumb-questions session, where we talked about college in general, STEM AP, and the [US] election. I'm so pleased that Kamala Harris and Joe Biden won. It's insane. I'm so happy. I can't wait to hear about the Peace Corps during this Monday's class. I've always been a little fascinated with the Peace Corps and I think it might be a nice way to center myself before going to graduate school. I don't know, but I'm glad I'll be able to hear about it on Monday. I have so many questions!"

The Future of the STEM AP Community

While responding to the impact of the pandemic, STEM AP also embarked on yet another transformation: transitioning from a formal, credit-earning program to a fully student-run organization. As is true for most STEM retention programs, ours was initially funded through grants and awards. We were fortunate to have early support from the highest level of our university administration, with a sizeable award from the president's office. These funds provided three years of valuable support as we searched for the perfect administrators, designed and tested our activities, and engaged our first cohort of students.

When it became clear that our program was filling a vital student need, we applied for funds from the National Science Foundation and were privileged to be granted a further three years of support from the Division of Undergraduate Education. These funds allowed us to increase the size of our program, as we began to more formally evaluate its impact. We employed pre- and post-program surveys to determine which aspect of the program had the greatest immediate impact on our students. We also spent time surveying alumni as they navigated their career paths after leaving college. One of the most valuable lessons we learned from these evaluation efforts was the importance our students placed on this program that belonged to them. They have eagerly taken ownership of almost every aspect of STEM AP over the past few years of its existence.

Although we continued to fundraise and consider novel avenues of formal support, it slowly became clear that our students had the motivation and passion required to take over this program and truly make it their own. The student leaders, although a bit anxious about losing some of the existing formal support the program offers, were keen to explore this possibility. They researched the process of forming a new student-run organization, or SRO, and created a timeline for submitting an application. They held elections to identify a president, vice president, and treasurer and prepared a prospectus that they shared with us, while inviting our input. To our surprise and delight, their vision of the STEM AP SRO looked remarkably like the formal program. These students wanted to recreate every aspect of the existing program in their new student-led organization! Even more encouraging was that they matched their ambitious vision with defendable goals and measurable milestones.

While waiting to learn about the fate of their SRO application, the students decided to forge ahead, informally, with their newly named "STEM Club." Since the COVID-19 pandemic was still in full force, the club had to exist solely online for its first semester. We were concerned that this nascent effort might be derailed by the impact of this virtual requirement. But once again, we were pleasantly surprised and encouraged by the fact that the club had more than 80 students apply for immediate membership!

We confess that it has been challenging to passively watch "our" program move on without us. But this momentary sense of loss is far outweighed by our pride in what these students have accomplished. They now literally "own" the STEM Ambassadors Program. What better way to ensure that students gain access to the resources they require? They know best what they need and have the passion and energy to push for access to the resources available. Research has shown that the most effective way to elevate student achievement is to empower them to take ownership of their learning.[5] These studies highlight the simple idea that if students don't believe what they do matters in terms of their learning and achievement, why would they be willing to put forth the effort to do hard things?[6] In our experience, this idea can be particularly important for URM students as they develop their self-efficacy in educational pursuits. This new model of academic development provides a more flexible approach to how we view a curriculum of study, one that harnesses students' agency and fosters a sense of belonging to a learning community. We see our students' decision to take ownership of the STEM AP as a critical attempt by them to develop their own culture of learning and to promote their own social connectedness and agency.

References

1. Thébaud, S.; Charles, M. Segregation, Stereotypes, and STEM. *Soc. Sci.* **2018**, *7* (7), 111. DOI:10.3390/socsci7070111.
2. Ong, M.; Smith, J. M.; Ko, L. T. Counterspaces for Women of Color in STEM Higher Education: Marginal and Central Spaces for Persistence and Success: COUNTERSPACES FOR WOMEN OF COLOR IN STEM EDUCATION. *J. Res. Sci. Teach.* **2018**, *55* (2), 206–245. DOI:10.1002/tea.21417.
3. Killpack, T. L.; Melón, L. C. Toward Inclusive STEM Classrooms: What Personal Role Do Faculty Play? *C.B.E. Life Sci. Educ.* **2016**, *15* (3). DOI:10.1187/cbe.16-01-0020.

4. van den Hurk, A.; Meelissen, M.; van Langen, A. Interventions in Education to Prevent STEM Pipeline Leakage. *Int. J. Sci. Educ.* **2019**, *41* (2), 150–164. DOI:10.1080/09500693.2018.1540897.
5. Bandura, A. Perceived Self-Efficacy in Cognitive Development and Functioning. *Educ. Psychol.* **1993**, *28* (2), 117–148. DOI:10.1207/s15326985ep2802_3.
6. Pym, J.; Kapp, R. Harnessing Agency: Towards a Learning Model for Undergraduate Students. *Stud. High Educ.* **2013**, *38* (2), 272–284. DOI:10.1080/03075079.2011.582096.

Chapter 6

Our Students' Voices

Our Alumni Speak

We have repeatedly stated how important it is to listen to your students (or employees) and invite them to share their concerns, challenges, and desires with you. If you only had the time, energy, or resources to spend on one single action in your efforts to engage and retain STEM students (or professionals), we would urge you to devote that time to listening. We spent seven years listening as our students reflected on their experiences in college and in our program. We have shared some of their thoughts with you in the prior chapters; perhaps their words have helped you appreciate why we felt compelled to write this book.

Our student's voices are powerful—more powerful than those of the faculty who teach them or the administrators who run our colleges. They have important messages for us to hear, which are often not what we anticipated.

And yet, where are those voices in the broader dialogue? The literature devoted to increasing STEM retention is massive, with thousands upon thousands of publications, books, and reports. Blogs and forums devoted to engaging educators in STEM retention abound. However, we looked high and low for websites or forums devoted to engaging these same students in telling their stories, and we couldn't find them. To be fair, there are certainly numerous organizations focused on increasing diversity in STEM and highlighting what students have accomplished, such as WISE[1] (Women in Science and Engineering), the International STEM Student's Forum,[2] and the WWT (World Wide Technology) Forum.[3] But when you dive into these resources, one rarely encounters the students themselves. Their voices are not the focus.

One of our goals in prior chapters was to introduce you to the diversity of our students, the diversity of their challenges, and the diversity of their reflections on the impacts of our program, all recorded in real time as they experienced their college journey. In this chapter, we invited several STEM AP alumni to look back and reflect on how, after leaving our program, they feel STEM AP impacted their STEM careers, their STEM identities, and their lives. We invite you to listen to their thoughts.

We triggered their reflections by asking the following question: How did your involvement in STEM AP enhance your college life and in what way did it create opportunities that contributed to your success? This may seem like a

Empowering Underrepresented Students in Science. DOI: http://dx.doi.org/10.1016/B978-0-323-90469-8.00006-8

leading question, making the assumption that STEM AP was a positive experience for them. However, we have typically spent nearly four years (sometimes more) with each of these students and have held numerous conversations about our program. Each was actively involved in STEM AP leadership roles and devoted considerable energy to making our program better able to meet our diverse students' needs. They speak with experience and authority about STEM AP.

Natalie

"Being a first-generation college student, my initial expectation for college was that it would be a slightly more intense version of the AP classes that I had taken in high school. It would only take the first few weeks of college to see that this was not the case. [Being] plunged into a new environment filled with competitive and highly accomplished classmates made me feel inferior and highly self-conscious. Most of my peers came from school systems that offered a plethora of AP classes and lab opportunities that put them at an advantage in seamlessly transitioning to college coursework. I remember feeling like I was always behind my freshman year. It was honestly frustrating, having to grapple with transcription and translation mechanisms in biology or the feelings of inadequacy in constantly struggling with stoichiometry in general chemistry. My inner fear of failure and deep feelings of impostor syndrome made it difficult for me to reach out and ask for help from others."

"When I first joined STEM AP, I did not have many expectations. Judging from the email sent to us before we started our freshman year, it seemed to be a minimal commitment type of a mentoring program. However, it caught my eye, and I am glad that it did. I remember at the first meeting, peering into a classroom filled with faces of every color. It was relieving to see diversity in a place that can seem monochromatic. I immediately felt at ease. STEM AP offered the space to form friendships with amiable and like-minded people who have similar upbringings and backgrounds. From informative forums to seminars on de-stressing, STEM AP has offered mentorship and camaraderie in an atmosphere that can often be aggressive and merciless. This innovative program also granted me my first exposure to lab research during the summer of my freshman year. My first research summer ultimately shaped how I investigate science and has led me to greater research opportunities throughout my college career."

"The mentoring experience at the Kelley Middle School in Holyoke will always be the proverbial seed that sprouted my passion to mentor. Seeing and experiencing the world through a different lens inspired me to pursue a mission trip to Leogane, Haiti, to volunteer at a free healthcare clinic. Being able to transform the lives of others while exposing myself to flagrant inequalities has sculptured [sic] who I am and the morals I believe in. The STEM Ambassadors Program was instrumental in confirming my interests in community and public health as an aspiring physician."

"I am thankful to STEM AP for the endless scope of possibilities that I had the chance to explore and the bottomless support from the members and the directors of the program. Being a part of a nurturing community that offered important opportunities and fostered lifelong relationships helped alleviate the challenging time that is college, and I am forever grateful."

Wei Li

"STEM AP has greatly enhanced my college life and created opportunities that contributed to my success. Without STEM AP, I would have dropped STEM in my second semester of my first year of college. I am a low-income first-generation college student. I received assistance applying to colleges through GEAR UP (Gaining Early Awareness and Readiness for Undergraduate Programs, a federal college preparation initiative). As a first-year student, I juggled work-study and classes. Nobody told me that working and taking classes would be difficult. I was in a College of Natural Sciences Residential Academic Program, meaning that most people on my floor were likely in the same classes as me. After exams, we would always get together and talk about the questions we struggled with and when we got our grades back, we went over it with each other. I consistently had lower grades than my peers and fell into comparison mode. I didn't take into account that they did not have jobs, so a majority of their time could be spent studying or reviewing lectures. Since I fell so deep into comparison, I contemplated quitting Biology or double majoring so that I had a plan B if I ended up not succeeding in Biology."

"The STEM AP director read my reflection about my contemplation to leave STEM and to create a plan B; she sent me an email saying that whatever decision I made would be okay, but that she would like to discuss it in person, so I made an appointment. We went over my grades and discussed where my contemplation was stemming from. She told me that my grades were good and told me that in creating the plan B, I was doubting myself. She knew why I chose Biology as a major, she knew my dream career of becoming a genetic counselor, and told me that in creating the plan B, I wasn't allowing myself to see my potential. I was preparing to settle rather than work as hard as I can to complete my degree to pursue my dream career. She referred me to a student she knew in the non-STEM major I had an interest in so I could learn more and make a more informed decision. I ended up not reaching out to the student, and took to heart what the director said to me; I decided to stick with Biology and put as much energy as I could into it for the sake of my dream career."

"STEM AP connected me to a research lab that I remained a part of for the rest of my undergraduate career and, now, for my graduate studies. The director of STEM AP encouraged me to apply to the Research Experience for Undergraduates (REU) because one of the PIs accepting students was studying genetics and because many students in STEM AP have found that research experience contributed to their success in STEM. The genetics lab was my first choice and I was ecstatic to hear that I had been accepted. My first summer in the lab was very overwhelming; there were so many techniques and terminologies to learn but I was grateful that my STEM AP REU group met weekly and discussed our experiences. We quickly learned that it was overwhelming for all of us and that it was normal to feel the way we did. By the end of the summer, we had a better grasp of our projects and our role in the lab. Lab gave me a deeper appreciation for the courses I was taking toward my Biology major. I got to dive deeper into some of the topics from my classes in the lab and it gave me purpose; it made me understand why those topics from class were important to know. While I still felt my academic performance was mediocre, conducting research in a lab encouraged me to continue my pursuit of my Bachelor's in Biology because it taught me that what I was studying had relevance. Prior to applying to this REU, I had searched for genetics labs, and the lab I joined through the REU never came up in my searches. If it were not for STEM AP, I never would have found or been a part of this lab."

"STEM AP was amazing because it gave me a multitude of opportunities to get to know small numbers of people, which allowed me to eventually get comfortable around everyone in STEM AP. For example, throughout my first year, I had two graduate mentors who I met with in a small group. There were four of us in this group and we got to talk about our majors as well as learn about how to read scientific articles and present figures. My middle school mentoring group became my close friends. There were three of us; we got to know each other better on the bus rides to middle school mentoring and we reflected on mentoring on our bus rides back to UMass. The summer of the REU after my first year, I had six people who I was meeting with every week, who I got to know better. This is now 13 very familiar faces by the end of my first year. In my second year, I was assigned a first-year mentee, who I would grab breakfast with biweekly, as part of our semester check-ins. As a second year [student], I learned how to pitch my research with my other second-year peers, so it allowed me to know people I might not have encountered in my first year. All of these encounters with smaller groups of people allowed me to be comfortable. I enjoyed the program so much that I could have presented to the entire room of 60-plus students because I was comfortable with around a third of them and because I loved the program so much and everything that they did for me. It wasn't long before I was given the opportunity to speak on my REU experience to the entire group, to share my story and to encourage the next wave of applicants."

"The summer after my third year at UMass, I was the undergraduate leader for the REU. I had the opportunity to lead a community of nine students (the most we had ever supported for the REU). Since it was a large group, I met with each student individually weekly to check in on their experiences in the lab and their experiences with their roommates. I was grateful I did those individual meetings, because the students trusted me enough to be honest about their experiences and struggles. We had whole-group events multiple times throughout the summer with nearly perfect attendance each time and provided fun ways to wind down within our community."

"My fourth year at UMass, I was approached by the directors of STEM AP to coordinate a symposium. As the student coordinator, I meet weekly with people to update them on the progress I had made and to discuss other tasks that needed to be accomplished. I sent emails to the guest speakers to coordinate their travel to UMass. I provided a template and feedback for posters for the symposium, and I edited and coordinated the printing of the posters. I edited and gathered all of the abstracts of the posters for the event brochure. I set up the posters prior to the event, captured pictures of the students as they presented, and collected notes on the talks by the guest speakers. I would have never imagined myself capable of coordinating that symposium if the directors did not tell me that they believed I was fit for the role. I was also able to speak on the stage about what STEM AP meant to me without feeling nervous, because STEM AP was my community and it was important to me that the guest speakers and symposium guests understood what STEM AP embodied, what STEM AP meant to me, and its impact on my life at UMass. STEM AP really made an effort to ensure you knew your peers. If I did not ever get to know my peers, I would not have felt comfortable in the program, and it would not have truly felt like community."

Lorenzo

"I joined the STEM Ambassadors Program during its early phases of development. As a first-generation, low-income, Pell Grant recipient, I had the odds of success stacked against me. With little academic and financial support from my parents, STEM AP provided a community that raised me up along people like myself. I was also able to uniquely engage with students from various communities, especially those from various racial backgrounds. After my freshman year, I was granted a research experience for undergrads (REU) that supported me financially while I worked in a lab on campus. It was this opportunity that has given me all that I have gained today. One small chance changed everything. STEM AP dramatically changed the trajectory of my life through strong mentoring, a commitment to raising equity, and advancing the self-efficacy of its students. I am so grateful."

"A central mission of STEM AP is to grow as a mentee and mentor. The mentorship I received through STEM AP-partnered graduate students gave me a diverse set of knowledge and skills. We dove deep into advanced scientific questions and were supported through the entire process. The greatest skill I learned was the belief in myself. I gained the belief that I am intelligent enough to engage with complex scientific topics. This was an amazing remedy to the feelings of idiocy I had from my introductory science courses. The 'weed-out' classes really damage students' sense of [their] abilities and intelligence. Along with a raised STEM self-efficacy, I was shown the power of research and higher education. Thanks to these mentoring partnerships, I have achieved my bachelor's degree and am on the path to receiving a master's, and desire to eventually achieve a PhD."

"Through the development of the STEM AP model, I was eventually placed into roles that required me to mentor other junior members. During my work as a mentor, I provided academic resources, research strategies, and the occasional socio-emotional support. I shared all my college survival tips. In this role, I learned what it means to commit to being a mentor, especially that it is not always easy nor convenient. Eventually, my propensity for building mentoring relationships extended outside of STEM AP, and I now currently maintain a network of students, my juniors, who often ask me for advice. I was the recipient of a fellowship that paid for a substantial part of my college tuition for one year. This was thanks to my previous experience in mentoring, due to STEM AP. I will be passing on the kindness of STEM AP and my mentoring experience for the rest of my life. It is extremely valuable for the success of students, especially from communities and backgrounds that face systematic oppression and barriers."

"STEM AP raised my awareness of social inequities. Talking with students of color, I heard their experiences with racial inequity on campus. Systematic racism and the inequitable treatment of students from low-income backgrounds is very apparent at the university and [especially] within the sciences. This inequity and intolerable unfairness is what brought our community even closer together. My time in the program has made me more aware and sympathetic to the struggle of racial injustice. I have had to face and identify my own racist upbringing and heal from the appalling system I was raised in. Developing real relationships with Black and Brown students aided in this endeavor of becoming not only 'not-racist' but also anti-racist. The progression of years in STEM AP was met with an ever-deepening desire to dedicate my existence to the movements of economic, environmental, racial, and social justice in society. Without intervention from a program like STEM AP, I am not sure how far along I would be in the process of unlearning racism. Without the existence of programs like STEM AP, disparities will continue to exist in academia at large."

"The blatant ignorance to the disparities one faces in life gives wealthy and white students an upper edge when getting involved in research. As a white low-income student, I saw that play out often in research labs. From anecdotal experience, many of the students accepted into labs are white, middle to upper class, honors college students with college-educated parents. From my experience, I saw privileged students had more chances at gaining experiences that make them more attractive to research labs. I was one of the only non-honors students in my lab, thanks to the intervention of STEM AP. I was likely not admitted to the honors college upon acceptance because of my high school grades. This standard of historically accepting honors students is unfair, as I was busy working a part-time job and keeping up with high school, something privileged students do not experience at the same rate. The inequity is likely even greater for students of color. My previously mentioned REU was a foot in the door to work in a lab that I remained with for more than three years. From my time, I have been able to get multiple co-authored research articles in prestigious journals. Lab-acquired skills and mentoring from this program has given me a leg up in my career. I have received multiple awards for my research."

"My experience in STEM AP will likely elevate my economic status in the future. The valuable opportunities I was afforded has enriched my life in many ways. I left STEM AP having an intensive research experience; deeper understanding of economic and racial injustice in the US; as well as skills in public speaking, community engagement, and education. In the 21st century, these competencies are key to success, I believe I am ahead of my peers of equal age in knowledge and experience in these areas. My involvement qualified me for a fellowship that has paid for a year and a half of my two years of graduate education."

"In whatever job I end up taking, the fundamental values of STEM AP will stay with me forever. I will work to raise the equity of my workspace. I will ensure proper inclusion of as many communities as possible. I will remain aware of racial injustice and economic inequity and the value that this perspective has in all communities. I am grateful for STEM AP. I deeply miss having constant contact with this community and will always support models such as this."

Santiago

"I remember as an incoming college freshman getting a letter from the STEM Ambassadors Program. It talked about how I would be working with a community of people and learning about the STEM field. It said that this was an opportunity for you to expand yourself and learn how to do research and gain experience for your future career in science. I was shocked and unsure if I should be a part of this community. I waited so long to press accept that it was the last day when I did so. I worked up the courage to finally email the program and accept my invitation. That was the best decision I have ever made. This program has nurtured me and helped me in every step of my journey, as I move[d] through my years in college."

"[I am] constantly looking for ways to improve my knowledge about science and continue my personal growth. The STEM Ambassadors Program has encouraged and pushed me to think creatively about science. It has pulled me further outside my comfort zone by putting me in situations where I had to meet new people and think about my future. They plant seeds for you to marinate in and think about. They do this by having speakers come in and talk about how they got into research and about how to reach your goals. They give you all the resources to be successful in this field. They don't just force you, or make you feel that because you are not at a certain point in your science career, you will not be successful. Instead, they push you and help you grow. This is what I have experienced as a STEM Ambassadors student. I have learned to push myself and ask for help when I need it. They taught me that it is healthy and important to talk about how you feel and to take time for yourself."

"I remember the first semester that I did the program, I participated in a CURE class, which was like an introduction to research and how to think like a scientist. I learned so much about myself. I gained confidence to speak out and lead a group. I also gained knowledge about a subject I did not know a lot about; most importantly, I learned that I can be a scientist. Science is what I love and where I want to be. This program has also allowed me to make connections with others. I learned about programs my peers were doing and how they got research opportunities."

"This program has also given me opportunities to be in positions of leadership. I participated in a peer mentoring program that allowed me to inspire kids to think and communicate with those around them. I also got to talk about my experiences with my peers and [about] certain classes and opportunities that are on campus. Overall, STEM [AP] has given me and many other underrepresented people in the science field an opportunity to feel seen, heard, and cared for. I have not only learned more about myself, but I have seen my peers grow in confidence. They inspire me to be better and to know that I can achieve anything I put my mind to. It is even more inspiring to know that these people look like me. They have been so successful in the STEM field and it is just so heart-warming to know that I will be among those people who have succeeded and reached their goal... all thanks to STEM [AP] and how much they nurture and care about every single one of their students. We are not just numbers on a sheet to them. We are people, and they go out of their way to know all of us and create a community where we help each other and spread information and knowledge."

Amira

"I blindly joined STEM AP my first year of college, [and] before [long] it quickly became a very important and valuable part of my college career. First and foremost, STEM AP provided me with lifelong friends, as it connected me with like-minded people with similar backgrounds and aspirations. Secondly, the program provided me with many mentoring opportunities, one of which allowed me to mentor middle school students from underrepresented communities in science. I was also mentored by third- and fourth-year college students during my first couple of years, and then eventually became a mentor myself to the younger cohorts. Thirdly, STEM AP matched me with a research laboratory of my choice during my first year, which not only provided me with the research experience I needed as a pre-medical student, but also opened my eyes to a new field of research that I currently love and work in post-graduation."

"However, my most valuable STEM AP experience came from being an undergraduate assistant at the STEM AP office. Being part of the program's staff gave me a sneak peek at all the planning and hard work that goes into creating and maintaining this effective program. Even just sitting in the office when I'm not in class, I got to engage in deep conversations that taught me a lot about modern racial, political, and even environmental problems that are in dire need of our attention. The program shaped me into the person I am today in every way possible, and I wish to take what I learned with me, wherever I go next."

"Being underrepresented at a big university can not only make you feel defeated and alone, but it can affect your school performance, as you won't have the same support and means as the other students in your classes. This program was created as a solution to connect you with similar people, as a safe place to discuss these worries and insecurities, and provide you with the support you need to perform your best. I had the rare opportunity of being supported by STEM AP as an underrepresented student in STEM, and also providing support and assistance to the other STEM students by being part of the program's staff. I will forever be grateful for this experience, as it introduced me to amazing students and mentors, taught me a lot about different groups of people and their hardships, and about different ways one is able to support and mentor their peers."

Shontelle

"A little over a year after my family's immigration to the United States, I was accepted to UMass Amherst. The summer prior to my commencement, I received an email from STEM AP offering a possible support for my transition to college as a STEM student. As a first-generation college student in this country, [I thought] this would be a great start to me finding my way."

"When I joined, I was able to connect with several peers who had similar interests, which was really exciting. We had workshops to enhance our academics, and did community outreach through middle school mentoring. Mentoring was a great opportunity to give back to a community in need but most importantly for me, to connect with and inspire those young minds." Some of the work I did start with mentoring students in the Holyoke middle schools to share with them how STEM is cool and possible for students like them, several of whom come from low-income families and are frequently people of color. At this time, the program was structured for what the administration thought the students needed, and in that first year and a half, STEM AP seemed like another class that I was taking.

"The turning point for me was when we got a new director and co-director who were women of color. Upon arrival, these individuals were committed to making the program for the students. From the first meeting, these women actually saw us individually for what we were. They brought their positive energy to our meetings and facilitated the building of a community that we lacked earlier. For me, this was extremely fundamental to my experience at UMass. STEM AP, ever since, became my home away from home. It was no longer a set of workshops to get me through school; it was a community to support me through this journey. The directors listened to us and put together workshops and activities that were essential for our inclusive and successful experience in STEM. The structures of the activities were appropriate for college level but not done in isolation, because each was carefully designed to facilitate connection to others. I really liked how some of these workshops were hosted and led by fellow STEM AP students, which I think was very empowering for them. With guidance from the leadership, upper-class students were able to design workshops tailored to the student experience, which I believe went so far. I personally was able to give one of the workshops on scientific presentation. Since I was in very similar shoes not long before, I felt that I connected more with the students' challenges and we worked through them together."

"Altogether, the student-led workshops and activities continued to connect us and build a community that empowered us to dream and do big."

"I also recall that when the new leadership arrived, the STEM AP office became a safe space for many. We came there to share our challenges, accomplishments, and dreams, or even just share a meal together. I grew closer to a lot of my colleagues along with our program directors and mentors in that space; something that many of us students appreciated."

"At the end of each week, we took time to reflect on our experiences both in STEM AP and our college experience at large. This was a really enlightening practice for me that I have brought with me [for] the rest of [my] life. It is through these reflections that we celebrate our accomplishments and recognize our weaknesses, which are essential to growth. Through the program, I was also positively impacted by the mentorship by peers and I continue to give back by mentoring underclassmen advancing through college. I will bring this practice of collaboration with me to support my peers as we navigate our next step: medical journeys and life together."

Wendy

"STEM AP defined my whole undergraduate college experience. I had no idea that it would become such a huge part of my identity when I applied to the program my freshman year. As a first-year student, I struggled with mental health issues. I ultimately had to take a medical leave during my first semester of my sophomore year. As I transitioned back to college after my semester-long leave, I increased my involvement in STEM AP. My involvement in the STEM Ambassadors Program is a big reason why I was able to create a positive college experience for myself after taking a medical leave."

"STEM AP surrounded me with a community for which I am extremely appreciative. As a person who struggles with mental health, it was tough to find a safe space in a large school like UMass Amherst. As I got increasingly involved in STEM AP, I gained friends and mentors whom I will always cherish. I spent countless hours in the STEM AP office, which was an inclusive and fun environment in addition to [being] a productive workspace. The students in STEM AP were from diverse backgrounds with varied perspectives. Through structured seminars and casual conversations in the office, I learned so much about culture and social issues. For example, much of my knowledge of the Black Lives Matter movement and microaggressions is due to what I learned in STEM AP. The directors were integral in creating the STEM AP community. Before they arrived, STEM AP was not fully developed and there was very little emphasis on connecting with other students. STEM AP flourished into a safe space for so many of us because of the efforts of these extraordinary women."

"I took on a leadership role in STEM AP during my third and fourth years at UMass. I helped organize and eventually lead other undergraduates in the Middle School Mentoring portion of the program. Middle School Mentoring comprises undergraduate mentors who serve as college role models for students in Grades 6-8. Mentors and mentees engage in after-school STEM enrichment activities and hands-on lab experiences. I created a curriculum for Middle School Mentoring by developing and adapting activities with a strong STEM focus that made learning fun. I often thought outside the box to create activities that maximized learning for everyone. It was a priority to make learning fun and accessible to all students. I am so grateful that I had the opportunity to take on a leadership role in this amazing part of STEM AP. Through this experience, I discovered that I love teaching. It was because of STEM AP and Middle School Mentoring that I decided to become a teacher. I am currently in graduate school pursuing my teaching licenses in Special Education and Elementary Education."

Alisha

"The UMass STEM Ambassadors Program was the first student organization I joined as an undergraduate. As a new student in a large school, it was comforting to be part of a smaller community. It was especially comforting to be among students with similar barriers to the STEM field as me."

"Had I not joined this group, I don't think I would be in the position I am today: applying to medical school and working in a research lab. In my sophomore year, when I felt that maybe I was not cut out for medicine, as a student with no family ever achieving graduate school, the program hosted a panel of current medical students who reassured me that it was possible. On days I felt that I was not competent enough to finish my thesis, I would walk into the STEM office and visit one of the directors, who are the heart of the program. I can attribute my success in completing courses and my thesis to one of the directors, Sonji, who always reminded me that simply my presence in these spaces was enough and necessary. As a current medical school applicant, I reflect on how fortunate I was to not only have support, but to be given insight into the barriers that other bright students have to higher education and how critical their presence is to effect life-saving change in medicine. I will forever be grateful for the confidence and purpose that the STEM Ambassadors Program community has instilled in me."

Navid

"I have been a part of STEM AP since December 2015. I continue to participate as a graduate student mentor. As a result, I have been in the program for nearly six years now. I graduated from UMass Amherst with a bachelor's degree in Informatics and Data Science in May 2019. I currently work as a data scientist and I am also a graduate student in the College of Information and Computer Sciences (CICS) at UMass. Throughout all of my courses in the computer science department, something that always bothered me was the sheer lack of Black students. I rarely ever saw peers that looked like me. Finding people who could resonate with the issues that are inextricably intertwined with being a Black student in computer science was unfortunately rare. The lack of underrepresented minority students in STEM is an issue that actively shapes the world. Without them, STEM fields lose the opportunity to incorporate the talent, ingenuity, perceptions, and insight that they undeniably have."

"STEM AP, however, was different. The number of students from all different backgrounds, races, and ethnicities was unreal and quite unlike anything I have ever experienced at UMass Amherst. When I convey my academic journey to undergraduates and other peers as a working professional today, one detail remains indelibly consistent: my participation in STEM AP changed my trajectory for the better, provided me with a community of amazing peers, and is a major factor for where I am today. As a graduate mentor, I am able to fill in the gaps that were glaringly apparent for me as an undergraduate student prior to joining STEM AP; at the same time, current students are able to rewrite and redefine historically inaccessible STEM spaces."

"Through workshops and activities that are meant to galvanize community among students of all STEM majors and backgrounds, STEM AP has managed to stick with me, countless alumni, and current students at UMass. Each week, when we met for the Monday night seminar, before we did anything else, the program director first ensured that the community had greeted each other and positively affirmed that what was coming next was not simply going to be good, but amazing. And amazing it was. The director and a panel of undergraduate students in the program worked together to provide offerings that compelled program members to pursue STEM careers, opportunities, and advanced degrees. Everything, from professional visits and summer scholarships to faculty sponsored research and leadership opportunities, was made possible by STEM AP."

"The directors are a pivotal pillar that helped bring the program to new heights since its inception. They did not merely see members as participants in the program; they saw everyone as people first. On countless occasions, the directors could be found sitting with students either during program sessions or at the program's office. They listened intently, commiserated when students needed space, and helped shed light on how to proceed in the dark. At the end of the day, the program directors and the student leaders made students like me feel seen. They made the program a safe space for everyone to learn more about STEM and, ultimately, feel like you belonged there."

"The program provided opportunities where the students themselves could lead each other through workshops, panels, and events. Every week, the directors greeted us with their warmth and easily defrosted the glacial barriers that prevent far too many Black people and people of color from participating, learning, and working in STEM-driven spaces. Subsequently, all students—from freshman to senior year—universally understood that they belonged, that they mattered, and that they were extremely capable."

"They also understood that they were STEM Ambassadors. As ambassadors, every single member is representative of their unique experiences and backgrounds in STEM. As members in the program and other communities throughout the world, every single member will carry their knowledge in a manner that inspires others to pursue and engage their own niche in STEM. These salient facts were instilled by the directors weekly and I am eternally grateful for that. Without STEM AP, UMass Amherst loses a major organization that has fostered a vanguard of alumni and current students that are tackling the world's challenges with deliberate and genuine intentions to make things better. Given the program's impact and its indisputable potential to grow, that is heartbreaking for me."*

Their Voices Matter

These alumni accounts attest to the point we have repeatedly made throughout this text. STEM Ambassadors see themselves represented in a STEM space; for many, it is the first time they have experienced a sense of belonging in STEM. They recognize the power of mentoring and being mentored. They value being invited to interact with program leaders and administrators and contributing to making the program meet their individual needs. These students recognize that they are the core of this community and that belonging to it has enabled them to forge meaningful friendships and relationships. They understand that their numerous reflections about themselves and the importance of their experiences—failures as well as successes—have helped them grow personally and professionally. All of these opportunities have provided these engaged and successful STEM scholars with a plethora of rich, life-changing experiences that have helped make them into the professionals and aspiring researchers, educators, and medical personnel they are today.

One critical perspective we gain from reading the words of these alumni is their recognition of the deliberate efforts made to create an inclusive, welcoming environment within which they were able to grow and thrive. We believe that this is the most notable accomplishment of our program. You hear from

*This reflection was recorded before the transition from the formal program to one led by students. We are happy to report that STEM club will continue in to the future.

our alumni that STEM AP provided them with a "safe space" in which they felt free to be themselves. More than any of the other opportunities our program has provided, our students cherish the feeling of belonging to something bigger than themselves and something in which they see themselves represented. STEM AP and all of its members have not only created an environment that contributes to the success of underrepresented minorities in STEM studies, we have created scientists impassioned to replicate diversity and inclusivity in the spaces where they work and study and do research. Our students are creating the change they wish to see in the world!

We must emphasize that the accounts of these students and their commensurate success are not a matter of coincidence or happenstance. They are the result of focused, intentional, careful visioning and planning by program administrators and student leaders. The belief that a more inclusive and equitable world is not only desirable but *possible* is the driving force behind the efforts of STEM AP. As we invite your engagement and encourage your attempts (however minimal) to create change in your own STEM space, we entreat you to dream with us of a world in which people of all stripes, persuasions, world views, and experiences have a place to make their equal contribution to the development of new knowledge and discovery, and the freedom to offer creative solutions to the myriad serious concerns that face humanity.

Student voices have great value in asserting their own needs, describing their own journey, and accounting for where they found success. We step back from speaking for our students and instead allow them to speak for themselves. We gave them the wherewithal to tell their own story as they experienced it and perceived its meaning in their lives. That is what we attempted to present in this chapter. Additionally, we deliberately asked past students of our program to speak out because, having already graduated, there is distance between their undergraduate experience and their experience today as working professionals or graduate students. It is their words, according to their perception and experience, that we honor in this chapter.

Although our program attempts to showcase how change may occur at the local "on the ground" level of the STEM space, our greater hope and intention is that this diversity for which we continue to quest becomes representative of the way STEM and STEM scholarship are done on a much larger scale. The more diverse the science community, the richer and more robust the ideas and solutions it puts forth.

References

1. *Women in Science and Engineering (WISE) Initiative*; Da Vinci Science Center. https://www.davincisciencecenter.org/wise-initiative/
2. *The International STEM Student's Forum*; Vocational Training Council. https://stem.vtc.edu.hk/en/event-info/highlight/detail/49
3. *World Wide Technology STEM Student Forum*. https://www.wwt.com/news/wwt-recognizes-future-tech-leaders-at-annual-stem-student-forum/

Chapter 7

Creating Your Own STEM Support Systems

Should You Create a STEM Support System at Your Institution?

Our experiences with the STEM Ambassadors Program have taught us that the key ingredient in a successful STEM support system is creating an inclusive, embracing, and safe community in which our students connect with their peers and are encouraged to bring their whole selves to the table. The students we target in our program are often the first to attend college in their families, which means that they enter academia without the knowledge resources necessary to help them navigate its vast terrain. As such, they have a much harder time acclimating to the college environment and finding the other resources necessary to help them progress. It may also be difficult to find a community to make college a warmer and more intimate experience. These initial negative experiences and the anxiety they generate can rapidly impact a student's college trajectory, slowing down their progress, limiting their opportunities, raising self-doubt, and resulting in discouragement. This is the story we hear from our students, time and time again.

We, at STEM AP, focus on the impact of this negative feedback loop on first-generation and URM STEM students, but it could equally apply to students of a similar demographic in any major; at any university, college, or community college; and in the workplace. The outcomes too will be similar: more of our first-generation and URM students will drop out, change majors, or simply never excel in their studies and professions to the levels they seek and are capable of achieving. The impact downstream—in our case, on diversity in STEM graduate studies, professionals, and the workforce—is not hard to imagine. Fewer students of color become PhD holders, medical doctors, academics, entrepreneurs, or research scientists; the list goes on, and on, and on.

We will continue to focus this conversation on students in an academic setting. However, it is absolutely the case that employees in the STEM workforce will share this same sense of otherness, hesitation, and anxiety when entering an environment in which they are perceived as the outsider, the minority, or the exception to the norm. Whether you are a faculty member at a university,

Empowering Underrepresented Students in Science. DOI: http://dx.doi.org/10.1016/B978-0-323-90469-8.00007-X

an administrator at a research foundation, or an employer in a STEM industry, the same holds true. Thus, to ensure we recruit and retain the greatest diversity of our students or employees, we must create environments designed for them to flourish. It is our deep hope that more than just faculty and college administrators will learn from our experiences as we all try to foster and encourage a more inclusive and inviting community in our classrooms, laboratories, or workplaces; one in which the resources that the students and employees bring, are celebrated and highly valued.

Appreciating the Importance of Creating a More Inclusive Classroom

One of the first steps toward change, as strange as this may sound, is to recognize the problem. We often hear from faculty that they are fully aware of the challenges of retention among first-generation and URM STEM students. When asked about their attempts to address this challenge, we hear that they are incorporating diversity into their lecture slides, or that they are pausing after asking a question to look beyond the first hand raised, or they are using pronouns appropriately. While these are all important and student-affirming actions, it is time we recognize the very large elephant sprawling and bellowing in the middle of our classrooms: many (dare we say most) faculty are uninformed about how truly critical this problem is, or they understand but feel powerless to do something about it.

From our perspective, the most important first step you, as teachers or employers, can take is to ensure that your classroom or workplace environment is inclusive and respectful of all students and employees. Research has shown that a positive classroom climate significantly improves persistence in college students, particularly URM and first-generation students.[1] In fact, employing inclusive teaching practices has a greater impact on student performance than do their own backgrounds.[2,3] Many faculty, however, have not yet learned how to address the critical factors of diversity and inclusion in the classroom. We often don't have the tools or know-how to find the resources that can help us enact a more inclusive teaching style. We may not even be aware of how our personal actions could negatively impact those very students we work so hard to engage.[4]

There is a rapidly growing literature on how inclusive excellence can be infused into our STEM classrooms.[4] To begin with, we acknowledge our own implicit biases and recognize that our students' experiences may differ significantly from our own; thus, they may have trouble integrating into the teaching style that feels so comfortable to each of us. If you have not yet done so, we urge you to take the time to examine your own privileges: those advantages you have experienced that make it more likely for you to find success in your own social system.[5,6] Consider how your own advantages have shaped the way you think, the way you act, and most relevant here, the way you run your classroom. Once you begin to recognize how you have created your own identity as a scientist, it becomes far easier to see how that process may not resonate with your students. The good news is that it doesn't take much to dramatically shift how your students view your educational efforts.

Taking the First Steps: Simple Ways to Create a More Inclusive STEM Classroom

Some of the most powerful actions you can take to create a more inclusive STEM classroom are fairly simple and inexpensive. We mentioned above that many instructors have realized that they need to change their portrayal of diversity in science and incorporate a more diverse set of images or examples to ensure students can more fully relate to the science world we present. Helping our students feel a sense of belonging to the scientific community has a critically important impact on persistence in STEM.[7] Old stereotypes linger and we must ensure that our students recognize that successful scientists are a diverse group; not all are old, white men.[8,9] Adrien Rich illustrates the power that stereotypes have on our students: "When someone with the authority of a teacher, say, describes the world and you are not in it, there is a moment of psychic disequilibrium, as if you looked into a mirror and saw nothing."[10]

One of our favorite approaches to creating a more inclusive classroom is to engage upper-level students to serve as undergraduate teaching assistants (UTAs) in our classes. Once a student has mastered the course material, they are very often eager to help future students navigate the course. If you ensure that your UTAs are representative of the diversity of your classroom, your students will see themselves in their UTAs and feel more confident that they, too, can succeed.[11] They may more easily connect with these role models and mentors than they do with the instructor, and these mentors may serve as precious lifelines as the younger students transition into college life.[12] These students may feel more comfortable asking questions of the UTAs; they may connect more readily with the UTA's approach to discussing the material and absorb more of the knowledge you want them to learn.[13] We have invited UTAs into all of our classes and have experienced a transformation in student engagement and the very quality of their work, and watched as our classrooms became more spirited and alive. Taking this very simple step can make an enormous difference to all of your students, but particularly to those who are underrepresented. Equally important is the fact that UTAs will gain the critical leadership experience that they crave and need to ensure they are well prepared for their own future STEM careers.[14]

A second, equally simple step toward inclusion is to make yourself a more authentic and approachable instructor.[4,15] Many of our students report that they don't attend office hours because the instructor appears so busy that they don't want to bother them. Others describe interactions with the instructor as being too stressful and thus, something to be avoided. Many of us may have had students who only appear at office hours once a situation is so serious that the student is in despair and considering dropping the course or, worse yet, leaving college entirely. Research makes it clear that our students value authentic instructors who make time for them, open up to them, and share their experiences and feelings.[15] Consider sharing your passion for your research in an informal seminar, bringing students into your research lab if you have one, or simply making yourself seem approachable and, yes, more human. Let your students see your vulnerable side: the fact that you, too, have failed exams or missed assignments, that there was a time when you were confused about your path in life and needed help from some insightful role model or mentor, or that you felt like an impostor, certain that you would be found lacking. Some of us have even used incentives, such as extra credit points, to get those students into our offices for the first time. Once they show up and realize that you are genuinely interested in what they have to say and respond to their concerns, then the magic begins!

One further simple approach to increasing inclusivity is to incorporate student reflection in your assignments. Invite students to connect the course materials to their own lives and experiences. When we promote reflective classrooms, we help ensure that students are fully engaged in the process of making meaning of the material we provide.[16] Instructors can ensure that the students are the producers, not just the consumers, of knowledge.

Although they may hesitate to share at first, many will come to relish this opportunity over time. You can even invite UTAs to model what you hope to achieve and share their reflections with their mentees. We have experimented with creating reflection forums where students contribute and are then invited to respond to their fellow students' submissions. In our experience, even a very large lecture class becomes instantly smaller as these students find others with similar experiences or perspectives as their own.

Some may be thinking about how remedial the steps we propose are. You might wonder why this conversation is even necessary. The actions we describe are all well-established, effective strategies to create more inclusive classrooms. And yet, it is important for the educators reading this text to understand that most university STEM professors were never trained to be educators. This material *is* new to them and, if adopted, represents a fundamental shift in how they think about educating their students. Most research scientists learned how to engage in science from within an apprenticeship system that promotes individuality and requires keen competition, while encouraging emulation of one's advisor. The term "inclusivity" is rarely uttered in such an environment. The incentives placed on faculty who emerge from these training programs are based upon their ability to maintain research funding and produce science publications. There is little to no attention paid to their teaching efforts. If they show up, offer their lectures, and produce grades for their students, that box is ticked on the tenure checklist. Our goal is to ensure that those not steeped in STEM pedagogy or trained to recognize racial disparity or even acknowledge their own implicit biases, can be encouraged to take the first steps toward creating a more inclusive classroom. We hope to inspire this audience with our own experiences and, even more importantly, provide the opportunity for them to hear directly from our students, as they tell us what they need to succeed as STEM students. Working toward inclusive excellence can truly be one of the most transformative steps you take in your STEM career.

Organizing a Supportive Community

After eight years of creating, refining, and supporting STEM AP, there came a moment when we had to determine the future trajectory of our program. We were well supported initially, with a generous start-up award from the university president's office and an equally generous grant from the National Science Foundation, to ensure that the program we developed was evidence-based, effective, and reproducible. With those funds, we engaged experienced educators to inform our program model and evaluation methods; we ensured all of our students had access to at least one significant research experience and provided summer REUs to many of our students; we offered skill development programs, transported mentors to middle schools, and hosted the occasional social event. Perhaps most important of all, these resources enabled us to hire two extraordinary directors, both women of color, who had the experience, personality, and talent to instantly connect with our students. These women were magnets—they drew in more students than we thought possible—all while serving as powerful positive role models of and providing the heart and soul to our community.

We recognize that the university and government funding permitted us to create something special, perhaps unique, in the STEM retention world. Our program was comprehensive, serving all of our students' needs as they developed their STEM identities and gained confidence and experience in their field and lives. These same students freely gave back to our program, serving as peer mentors and in leadership roles. In fact, one of the greatest surprises of our program came straight from the students: their eagerness to be involved, to give back to the community, to bring others into the fold.

The true test of our community occurred when we made the decision to close the formal program, primarily due to lack of future funding. We approached our students one year in advance of this pending closure and spent many hours discussing our decision and helping them understand why we felt forced to move in this direction. Our reasons for ending the program are varied—some quite personal, and still others simply due to the lack of continued commitment by the university. It still seems strange to us that the university would make such a significant investment to develop this program, which was then matched by an equally significant investment by the NSF, only to later choose not to commit the resources required to ensure the survival of this highly successful program. To be fair, the university has made numerous, significant investments in STEM retention. A variety of innovative and compelling programs have been created and tested.

However, when we state that our program was highly successful, we speak from the students' perspectives. You have heard a small sample of their voices and recognized their passion for this program. It is also true that once established, STEM AP engaged more students per year than all other STEM retention programs on the campus combined. We had an open-door policy that welcomed all comers, in sharp contrast to most campus-based retention programs that require applications and competition for very limited numbers of participants. Our students cherish that we deliberately chose not to limit our numbers. They craved admission to a community that was not exclusive, that welcomed all, regardless of their GPAs, and that didn't require them to compete for access to this precious resource.

Our students were predictably devastated by our decision to end the formal program and tried very hard to convince us to reconsider. However, once the community accepted that our reasoning was sound, an extraordinary transformation occurred. This close-knit community of more than 100 active STEM participants and an equal number of alumni, decided they would not let this program disappear. They spent several months developing a proposal to transition STEM AP into a student-led club. They formed a leadership team and drafted a document of intent. They elected a president and agreed upon formal bylaws. Just recently, we were provided with a syllabus for their inaugural semester. It is almost identical to the syllabus of the formal program; except now, it is being offered and supported solely by students! They will have little to no funding for this effort, save for the small stipend offered to all college clubs, and yet, our STEM Ambassadors are undaunted, determined to keep their community intact. That is what we mean when we state that STEM AP is a highly successful program: our students themselves are determined it will not end.

It is too early to know if this club-based approach to STEM AP will survive, much less succeed at the high level we have already seen. It will certainly require significant dedication by the students; something that, at least, does not appear to be in short supply. However, regardless of the future of the STEM AP club, this compelling need to ensure the survival of their community is a clear indication of the importance it holds in our students' lives. They need community; they require it as much as they require access to their courses, a safe place to sleep, and healthful food to eat. They crave this community; it provides a critical support system, one they feel so strongly about that they are willing to take significant steps to ensure its promulgation. They love this community; we continually receive a stream of emails from current and former students thanking us for the "gifts" we provided them and explaining how this program changed their lives' trajectories. We frequently remind them that they gave us gifts of even greater value!

How can more of us enable and support the creation of these types of student communities on our campuses or workplaces? Well, to start, you do not need to replicate STEM AP. Your first step might be to identify several students you feel might benefit from such a community and invite them to visit your office or lab. We find offering a pizza lunch or an ice cream social will usually inspire enough students to attend.

Your role then transitions to that of a listener. Don't try to direct the conversation; let the students open up and share their thoughts if and when they are ready to do so. Let them take charge of the conversations. Let them just sit and eat, if that is what they need. What we have repeatedly observed is that over time, the students will start to ask you questions, perhaps strictly professional at first, but eventually, they may ask about your life's journey. *This* is your moment, the chance to become more human in their eyes. Share things that you failed at, that didn't work the way you expected, or those times you felt insecure. Also, share your inspirations and accomplishments, but don't focus only on your success. It is critical that your students recognize that you are human, that you have struggled and failed, even if you now run a successful lab or hold a prestigious position at the university. Help them realize that, even if you come from a position of privilege, you are a caring and empathetic person who has had your own unique journey in life. The students may not instantly accept you. The process of instilling trust requires patience and commitment on your part to prove to these students that you care about them and want to help them succeed in their endeavors.

This simple act may be all you can provide, and, if so, it is absolutely enough. A cohort of students will be inspired by your attention and be slightly more likely to survive their STEM studies. What a wonderful opportunity that you provided, for the mere price of a pizza and some of your time. However, and this is only for those willing to invest a bit more time and a bit more commitment, you may be able to urge the students to transform these meetings into something more. Perhaps they create a study group, or a journal club, or a career panel, or whatever other ideas they propose. The focus of the group is not important; what is key is that you are listening to them and supporting them in their endeavor.

Our program started with 35 students and very little of the organization we have described in such detail above. The fact that the students had a program devoted to them—one targeting URM and first-generation college STEM students—was enough to get them through the door. Once engaged, they helped us make the program what it is today. We listened more than we spoke and we followed up on their ideas. We didn't always provide what they asked for, but we acknowledged their needs and did the very best we could to meet them. The result is a community so committed to our program that they simply won't let it end. We are very proud that our students have taken charge of the program and are transforming it into precisely what they want and need. Although we must confess it is hard to let go of the reins, this gradual transition from faculty-inspired and -led to student-run has been ongoing for several years and we are excited to watch the continued evolution of STEM AP.

The Top-Down Approach: The Role of Institutes of Higher Education

Institutes of higher education have a key role to play in ensuring that all STEM students can thrive and excel in their studies. At a conference devoted to this subject, Jerry Kang, the vice chancellor of equity, diversity and inclusion at the University of California, Los Angeles, noted: "The value of inclusion is not just because we want to be kind and nice and warm, though those are important things. But inclusion and social belonging leads people to perform to their highest capacity."[17]

And this is not just about STEM. The challenges of minority STEM students converge with their broader experiences on a predominately white campus.[18] To effect change and create a more diverse and inclusive community of scholars, academic institutions must develop long-term strategies that can be quantitatively evaluated to ensure that measurable progress is being made. Cosmetic compliance due to ever-changing political pressures will not suffice.

But where do colleges and universities even start this transformation? Damon Williams a leading authority on educational achievement and inclusive excellence, suggests that we need strategic diversity leadership that can shift from our current paradigm, in which the focus is primarily on protecting the rights and enhancing the opportunities of historically disadvantaged individuals, to one that recognizes that to succeed in the 21st century, our academic institutions must achieve academic excellence and position themselves to compete successfully in the global market.[19]

We will touch on only one aspect of this challenge for academic leadership. Many research universities have created a two-track system, in which the STEM "research" is done by scientists, while the STEM "teaching" is done primarily by lecturers. In this model, research scientists are evaluated based upon their success in raising research funds and publishing articles, whereas lecturers are evaluated based upon their teaching approaches and the number of students they teach. This disconnect between the research and teaching is damaging on many fronts. It results in far greater prestige and praise lavished on the successful researcher, while a different lens is focused on the lecturers, one that has far fewer avenues to achieve recognition and is accompanied by far lower salaries. This model is also damaging to the students. It does not require or incentivize research scientists to improve their teaching and it results in far fewer students having the opportunity to interact directly with research-active STEM faculty. Further, it does not explicitly acknowledge that reaching the levels of STEM retention we seek requires a fundamental change in cultural attitudes about teaching; a shift that recognizes that excellent teaching requires skill and training.[20] Promotion and tenure packages for research scientists rarely assess or even acknowledge teaching quality or educational scholarship efforts.

We created STEM AP because of the great need we saw among our students, particularly first-generation and URM students. These students weren't connecting with our lecture materials and were choosing not to access resources that we thought they needed. Initially, we tried a simple experiment: invite these same students to mentor middle school students. The response was overwhelmingly positive. In an instant, we had a passionate team of first-year undergraduates devoting some of their precious time to travel to local schools and engage the youth in science. From that very first step, we have watched STEM AP grow, diversify its approaches, and attract and retain a diverse body of STEM students who are passionate about this program. We were fortunate to have a dean who very quickly saw the potential of our program and successfully fought on our behalf to obtain the financial support required to get STEM AP off the ground.

We recognize that not every faculty member, department, or university will have the inclination, the passion, or the time to create their own version of STEM AP, much as we would love to see that outcome! Our primary goal with this book, then, is two-fold. First, we want our readers to hear directly from students what they need to succeed in their STEM studies. Second, we provide numerous examples of how we have responded to our students' needs, with the expectation that readers may connect with one or more of our suggestions and make changes in their own educational approaches. Our students crave a supportive community; they want to see themselves represented in the science world we present to them; they want to feel encouraged to speak up and have their voices heard and appreciated. None of these needs are expensive, nor do they require the formal programs we created in STEM AP. Taking even a few of the simpler steps will result in a more inclusive classroom that can make all the difference to your students.

One of the most valuable aspects of STEM AP, from our students' perspective, is the community we created. Intentionality is a critical component in the design and implementation of our community. We *intentionally* designed a community to improve the academic success and career preparation of URM and first-generation college students.[21] Our students benefit from having a culturally supportive environment that provides easily accessed resources. These same resources may already be offered by the university, but for many reasons, students of the demographic our program targets, either fail to find them or are reluctant to use them. When provided in an intentionally inclusive environment, though: voila, the students seek these same resources and use them with relish! University administrators must be aware of this challenging dilemma. It is not only the resources themselves that our students need. They need them to be provided in a format that encourages all students to access them.

Challenging institutional climates present real barriers to URM students. Most institutions recognize the value of multicultural engagement and the benefits of recruiting a diverse faculty but lack the will to ensure that these efforts are integrated into an environment of respect, inclusion, and engagement.[22] Efforts to improve institutional climates must start with honest assessments of current climate and environmental barriers.[23] Just as we invited faculty to examine their own privileges and how those experiences contributed to their development of themselves as scientists, so too must academic administrators determine the climate within their institutions and what roles they play in consciously creating a supportive climate.[24] Emphasis must be placed on identifying what messages our institution is sending and what values we are promoting. It is not enough to wave a banner that states "we value diversity"; it must be paired with deliberate actions to ensure we achieve diversity in some quantifiable manner.

There is reason for optimism that we are moving more rapidly than ever before in the direction of the institutional changes we desire. The rising costs of higher education have brought the issue of education quality and equity to the attention of politicians. Former President Obama engaged educators and STEM researchers in conversations about how to improve higher education, including a focus on monitoring and publishing student graduation and employment rates.[25] What better way to incentivize academic institutions to focus resources on quality teaching and student retention than to publish their success in meeting realistic goals of retention?

So Many Moving Pieces

One of the early directors of STEM AP felt overwhelmed when she first joined our program. "There are so many moving pieces to this program. How will we keep track of all the students and their needs?" It was a good question then, when we were just starting out, and it remains our greatest challenge: keeping in touch with each student; recognizing when they need help; and ensuring they gain access to all of the resources we at STEM AP, and the university as a whole, provide.

We believe that the answer to this question lies in the creation and support of a student-centered community in which students have equitable access to a diverse menu of resources specifically designed to support their academic success. That is clearly a tall order, but one that we argue is far more achievable than it seems at first blush. Our experiences in developing STEM AP have proven to us that the most successful STEM retention programs are designed based upon listening to students' needs, rather than providing a one-size-fits-all prescription. Some students need a peer mentor from their first days in college in order to rapidly acclimate to the university environment. Others require a stronger connection forged between their lives and the STEM subjects they study. And still others will benefit most from a CURE-based research experience rather than a laboratory-based one because they are not yet self-confident enough to promote themselves as a valuable member of a laboratory community. Once these same students realize that they are not alone, that there are others experiencing similar struggles and challenges, the hurdles seem smaller, the work less onerous, and their instinctual curiosity and passion emerge.

Additionally, and quite significantly, the efforts we make in having our students reflect on their own journeys—owning their own stories of struggle and using the encouragement that comes from those difficulties or successes to arm themselves for the challenges ahead—have proved most valuable to the development of their STEM identities. Through it all, our students learn to trust and respect themselves as scholars because they see the link between the science they came to university to pursue and their whole lives as human beings and citizens of the world. We work with our students to help them realize their potential; they cannot be the best scientists they could be without understanding the value of who they are in the world. Owning and embracing all of themselves imbues them with self-confidence and self-acceptance. Our world will benefit exponentially from the discoveries and the problem-solving acumen of scientists who are in tune with who they are, and who truly understand the impact of science on the lives of ordinary people—ordinary people like them. And ordinary people constitute most of the world. Ordinary people come beautifully varied, creative, and differently brilliant. Because it is in our best interest as a species to do so, science labs, classrooms, and industry spaces should expect and reflect this variety!

Finally, we must not ever lighten the pressure upon colleges and universities to do better about creating room in academia that is intentionally inclusive. Though it persists in far too many academic spaces, ignorance (or is it apathy?) of the need for inclusivity and equity must not persist, and therefore, must not ever be excused and passed off as the innocuous sounding "traditional approach." The "traditional approach" is antithetical to equity, diversity, and inclusivity. In addition to broadcasting their verbal proclamations about making campuses more diverse, universities and colleges must commit to *doing* what must be done to accomplish this crucial goal. Without the will to change, programs like STEM AP, no matter how provably remarkable, effective, and simple to implement, will not make it into the mainstream of academia. Students are willing to learn and be guided to do what they must, to create environments that will help them succeed, but they cannot realize this goal without the will, the desire, and the funds universities and colleges must invest to ensure its success. We used the funds and the resources made available to us to create a vibrant community of brilliant, innovative, diverse scientists. But before a dollar was ever spent to this end, there was the *desire* and the *will* to see students of varying backgrounds, who were traditionally underserved, succeed. The will and the desire for equity and inclusivity are what launched our program. We hope, most sincerely, that it may be that which launches and expands yours.

References

1. Cabrera, A. F.; Nora, A.; Terenzini, P. T.; Pascarella, E.; Hagedorn, L. S. Campus Racial Climate and the Adjustment of Students to College: A Comparison Between White Students and African-American Students. *J. High Educ.* **1999**, *70* (2), 134–160. DOI:10.1080/00221546.1999.11780759.
2. Cabrera, A. F.; Colbeck, C. L.; Terenzini, P. T. Developing Performance Indicators for Assessing Classroom Teaching Practices and Student Learning. *Res. High Educ.* **2001**, *42* (3), 327–352. DOI:10.1023/A:1018874023323.
3. Colbeck, C. L.; Cabrera, A. F.; Terenzini, P. T. Learning Professional Confidence: Linking Teaching Practices, Students' Self-Perceptions, and Gender. *Rev. High Educ.* **2001**, *24* (2), 173–191. DOI:10.1353/rhe.2000.0028.
4. Killpack, T. L.; Melón, L. C. Toward Inclusive STEM Classrooms: What Personal Role Do Faculty Play? *C.B.E. Life Sci. Educ.* **2016**, *15* (3). DOI:10.1187/cbe.16-01-0020.

5. Johnson, A. G. *Privilege Power, and Difference*, 3rd ed.; McGraw-Hill Education: New York, NY, 2018.
6. Kerr, B. A.; Multon, K. D.; Syme, M. L.; Fry, N. M.; Owens, R.; Hammond, M.; Robinson-Kurpius, S. Development of the Distance From Privilege Measures: A Tool for Understanding the Persistence of Talented Women in STEM. *J. Psychoeduc Assess.* **2012**, *30* (1), 88–102. DOI:10.1177/0734282911428198.
7. Gibbs, K. D.; McGready, J.; Bennett, J. C.; Griffin, K. Biomedical Science Ph.D. Career Interest Patterns by Race/Ethnicity and Gender. *PLoS One* **2014**, *9* (12), e114736. DOI:10.1371/journal.pone.0114736.
8. Hurtado, S.; Newman, C. B.; Tran, M. C.; Chang, M. J. Improving the Rate of Success for Underrepresented Racial Minorities in STEM Fields: Insights From a National Project. *New Dir. Inst. Res.* **2010**, *2010* (148), 5–15. DOI:10.1002/ir.357.
9. Finson, K. D. Drawing a Scientist: What We Do and Do Not Know After Fifty Years of Drawings. *Sch. Sci. Math.* **2002**, *102* (7), 335–345. DOI:10.1111/j.1949-8594.2002.tb18217.x.
10. Wheeler, L. *Diversity and Inclusive Teaching Practices in STEM*; Center for Teaching Excellence, University of Virginia: Charlottesville, VA, 2020.
11. Borem, A.; Smith, C. Developing and Supporting STEM Undergraduate Teaching Assistants as Partners in Teaching. in IEEE Frontiers in Education Conference (FIE); IEEE Publications: Uppsala, 2020; Vol. 2020, pp. 1–9. DOI:10.1109/FIE44824.2020.9274088.
12. Luckie, D. B.; Mancini, B. W.; Abdallah, N.; Kadouh, A. K.; Ungkuldee, A. C. P.; Hare, A. A. Undergraduate Teaching Assistants Can Provide Support for Reformed Practices to Raise Student Learning. *Adv. Physiol. Educ.* **2020**, *44* (1), 32–38. DOI:10.1152/advan.00090.2019.
13. Zaniewski, A. M.; Reinholz, D. Increasing STEM Success: A Near-Peer Mentoring Program in the Physical Sciences. *Int. J. S.T.E.M. Educ.* **2016**, *3* (1), 14. DOI:10.1186/s40594-016-0043-2.
14. Schalk, K. A.; McGinnis, J. R.; Harring, J. R.; Hendrickson, A.; Smith, A. C. The Undergraduate Teaching Assistant Experience Offers Opportunities Similar to the Undergraduate Research Experience. *J. Microbiol. Biol. Educ.* **2009**, *10* (1), 32–42. DOI:10.1128/jmbe.v10.97.
15. Johnson, Z. D.; LaBelle, S. An Examination of Teacher Authenticity in the College Classroom. *Commun. Educ.* **2017**, *66* (4), 423–439. DOI:10.1080/03634523.2017.1324167.
16. Baird, J. R.; Fensham, P. J.; Gunstone, R. F.; White, R. T. The Importance of Reflection in Improving Science Teaching and Learning. *J. Res. Sci. Teach.* **1991**, *28* (2), 163–182. DOI:10.1002/tea.3660280207.
17. The University World News Home Page: https://www.universityworldnews.com/post.php?story=20190712071639621 (accessed 2021-01-15).
18. Griffin, K. Addressing STEM Culture and Climate to Increase Diversity in STEM Disciplines. *Higher Education Today*. April 23, 2018. https://www.higheredtoday.org/2018/04/23/addressing-stem-culture-climate-increase-diversity-stem-disciplines/
19. Williams, D. A. *Strategic Diversity Leadership*; Stylus Publishing: Sterling, VA, 2013.
20. Suchman, E. L. Changing Academic Culture to Improve Undergraduate STEM Education. *Trends Microbiol.* **2014**, *22* (12), 657–659. DOI:10.1016/j.tim.2014.09.006.
21. Committee on Closing the Equity Gap: Securing Our STEM Education and Workforce Readiness Infrastructure in the Nation's Minority Serving Institutions; Board on Higher Education and Workforce; Policy and Global Affairs; National Academies of Sciences, Engineering, and Medicine. In; Espinosa, L. L., McGuire, K., Jackson, L .M., Eds. *Minority Serving Institutions: America's Underutilized Resource for Strengthening the STEM Workforce*; National Academies Press: Washington, DC, 2019, p 25257. DOI:10.17226/25257.

22. Price, E. G.; Gozu, A.; Kern, D. E.; Powe, N. R.; Wand, G. S.; Golden, S.; Cooper, L. A. The Role of Cultural Diversity Climate in Recruitment, Promotion, and Retention of Faculty in Academic Medicine. *J. Gen. Intern. Med.* **2005**, *20* (7), 565–571. DOI:10.1111/j.1525-1497.2005.0127.x.
23. Thompson, N. L.; Campbell, A. G. Addressing the Challenge of Diversity in the Graduate Ranks: Good Practices Yield Good Outcomes. *C.B.E. Life Sci. Educ.* **2013**, *12* (1), 19–29. DOI:10.1187/cbe.12-04-0054.
24. Bianchini, J. A. Expanding Underrepresented Minority Participation: America's Science and Technology Talent at the Crossroads: Book Reviews. *Sci. Ed.* **2013**, *97* (1), 163–166. DOI:10.1002/sce.21032.
25. The White House Blog Home Pate: https://obamawhitehouse.archives.gov/blog/2016/02/11/stem-all (accessed 2021-01-15).

Index